Solidworks 2019 Training Guide

Mechanical Design Concept

By

Linkan Sagar

FIRST EDITION 2019

Copyright © BPB Publications, INDIA

ISBN: 978-93-88511-79-7

Distributors:

BPB PUBLICATIONS
20, Ansari Road, Darya Ganj
New Delhi-110002
Ph: 23254990/23254991

BPB BOOK CENTRE
376 Old Lajpat Rai Market,
Delhi-110006
Ph: 23861747

MICRO MEDIA
Shop No. 5, Mahendra Chambers,
150 DN Rd. Next to Capital Cinema,
V.T. (C.S.T.) Station, MUMBAI-400 001
Ph: 22078296/22078297

DECCAN AGENCIES
4-3-329, Bank Street,
Hyderabad-500195
Ph: 24756967/24756400

Published by Manish Jain for BPB Publications, 20, Ansari Road, Darya Ganj, New Delhi-110002 and Printed by Repro India Pvt Ltd, Mumbai

Preface

This book carriers a lot for you if your starting solid work this book is extremely simple to understand. My vigorous effort toward the understanding of students and their problems in solidWorks. Mechanical engineer will be solved after my attempt for this book. So far, my earlier book AutoCAD 2015 references and then Autocad 2017 references followed by Autocad2018 ,3DMAX 2019, Revit 2019, Autocad2019, and now solidworks 2019 references have been a success for my beloved reader. As I receive positive feedback, and numerous peoples are benefitting from it, I am being more eloquent for this book with novel project and easy language. This book carries a lot for you If you are starting solidworks for the first time. This book is extremely simple understand and will enlighten you with fundamental of solid works. You can easily learn solidworks as it is a basic book, everything is explained in this in step by step form. The main objective of writing this book, after being inspired from my previous edition, is to make student enthusiastic about learning the concept of solidworks I wish you a great future in designing.

Acknowledgment

While writing this book, I was constantly supported and guided by many wonderful people. Their extended support will always be priceless for me. My mother, Archana Sagar, is a woman of substance. Like any other mother in the world, her unconditional support, caring nature, never-ending faith in me, and motivation encouraged me to finally realize that I can transfer my knowledge through writing for various other people who seek the same knowledge. And, this is how my book writing began. I would like to thank my sister, Shivani Sagar, who always lovingly supports, motivates, and inspires me. Many thanks to my wife, Mansi Sagar, who is a wonderful partner, she not only understands my dreams and aspirations, but is equally involved in internalizing and living it up with me. It's wonderful how she was took on all the responsibilities.

so that I can get space and comfort for writing this book with dedication. She stands strong with me in all the highs and lows of my life. These two women are the sources of continuous energy that keep me going. This book is about technical skills precision and perfection in the engineering field. My special thanks to Konica and Sonam who helped me to write this book in very short period of time, as I understand the technical aspect, but was unable to express.

And, last but not least, thanks to **BPB Publications**.

About the Author

Linkan Sagar has done B.tech from UPTU, Lucknow. He has extensively worked on various software like solidworks , catia, staad-pro, and revit. He is having wide industry experience and worked on more than 18 major live projects. He has delivered approximately 280 presentation in sector of engineering and designing.

Table of Content

CHAPTER 1

Introduction and Overview

What is SolidWorks?

SolidWorks is a product of Dassault System. It is a software which is used for Mechanical Modelling Aided Designing. It is used in designing like Sketching, Part designing, Surface, Sheet Metal, Mold Design, and Weldment, and so on. Also, it came into use in November 1995.

Name/Version	Version Number	Version History Value	Release Date
SolidWorks 95	1	46	November 1995[8]
SolidWorks 96	2	270	Early 1996
SolidWorks 97	3	483	Late 1996
SolidWorks 97Plus	4	629	1997
SolidWorks 98	5	817	1997
SolidWorks 98Plus	6	1008	1998
SolidWorks 99	7	1137	1998
SolidWorks 2000	8	1500	1999
SolidWorks 2001	9	1750	2000
SolidWorks 2001Plus	10	1950	2001
SolidWorks 2003	11	2200	2002
SolidWorks 2004	12	2500	2003
SolidWorks 2005	13	2800	2004
SolidWorks 2006[9]	14	3100	2005
SolidWorks 2007	15	3400	2006
SolidWorks 2008	16	3800	July 1, 2007
SolidWorks 2009	17	4100	January 28, 2008
SolidWorks 2010	18	4400	December 9, 2009
SolidWorks 2011	19	4700	June 17, 2010
SolidWorks 2012	20	5000	September, 2011
SolidWorks 2013	21	6000	September, 2012
SolidWorks 2014	22	7000	October 7, 2013
SolidWorks 2015	23	8000	September 9, 2014
SolidWorks 2016	24	9000	October 1, 2015
SolidWorks 2017	25	10000	September 19, 2016
SolidWorks 2018	26	11000	September 26, 2017

Figure 1 SolidWorks version list

Stating of SolidWorks?

A new tab is open when SolidWorks get started. There are three types of pages, first is **Part**, second is **Assembly**, and third is **Drawing**. If you want to create any part like Part, Surface sheet metal or any part of weldment so you can clock on Part. If you have already created many parts and now you want to assemble them to create a single product you can select assembly option. If you want to give details of drawing and you want to show that drawing, then select **Drawing** tab. If you already have a file and you want to open it then select **pen** option to easily open the file. You can open any type of file, it may be of **Part**, **Assembly** or **Drawing**.

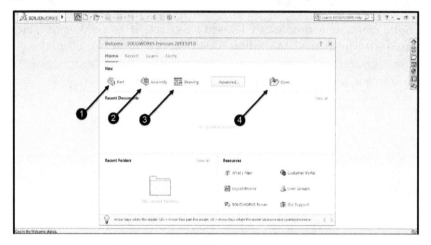

Figure 2 SolidWorks starting page

GUI of SolidWorks

1. **Menu Bar**: It is a normal toolbar. All tools are there in it. There are many tools like **File, Edit, View, Insert, Tools**, and so on. Usually it is used to find those tools which you cannot find out elsewhere, but you can find in this **Menu** bar.

2. **Quick access tool**: It is used to use some tools which are used mostly for short time. You can do all the settings of SolidWorks like page setup.

3. **Command Manager**: It is present in Ribbon bar, there are every tool present which are used to create drawing. There are many different

tabs like **Sketch**, **Features**, **Surface**, Sheet metal and Weldment, and so on. When you work on any Module, you can select the required tab and if there is no module you can right click on the tab and you can select any module which you want.

4. **Feature Manager Design Tree**: Design tree is used to create or modify design. It has advantage that you can modify the tool of any design, sketch or tool of module used in it.

5. **Status bar**: Status bar is used as command bar which helps in telling the steps.

6. **Unit:** You can set the unit for drawing directly from here.

7. **Graphics area:** Graphic area is a drawing area which is used to create the drawing.

8. **Resources:** It is used for the library of material, view palette and design.

9. **View toolbar:** View toolbar is used to show view of page or design view like view side, section view and visual style, and so on.

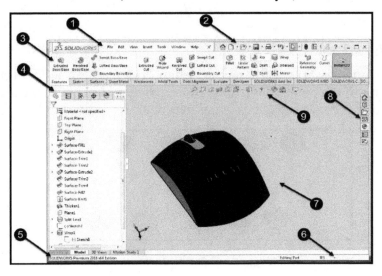

Figure 3 gui with number

Mouse Handling

Mouse has many works in SolidWorks like to move the page, to zoom in or zoom out and it has an important role to click.

1. Left button is used to select the object, or you can click anywhere.
2. The right button is used to get additional options such as hiding the object and the normal view option.
3. Scroll is used to zoom in or zoom out the page, by scrolling it forward or backward.
4. Scroll is also used to rotate the page by pressing and moving it.

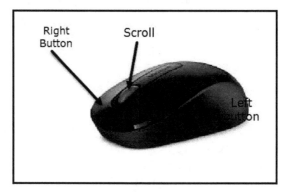

Figure 4 Mouse button

View Tool

View toolbar is used to change the setting of view style of design of current page. It can change the settings of view style of design like section part, side view of design and its visual style of it.

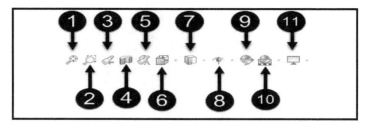

Figure 5 View tool with number

1. **Zoom to fit**: It is used to fit the drawing in drawing area.

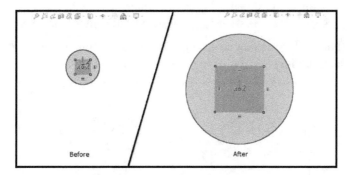

Figure 6 Zoom image

2. **Zoom to area**: It is used for zooming that particular area which you want to zoom. For this, first you need to select the first corner of that area and then the opposite one.

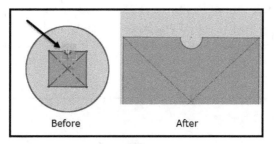

Figure 7 Zoom area image

3. **Previous view:** It is used to change the current view to get the previous view. Suppose you create a sketch and set the front view for this and you rotate the sketch now you want to see the front view so you can click on front view icon to see that view.

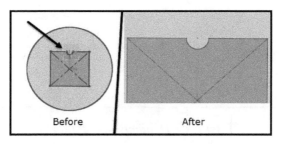

Figure 8 Pervious view image

4. **Section view:** It is used to get the interior view of any part by cutting it. Section can be seen from any view like any plane or side view.

   (**Note:** If you want to change the plane, you can change it from the section view tab.)

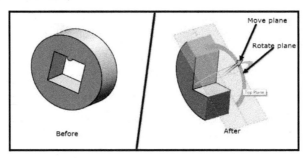

Figure 9 section view

5. **Dynamic annotation view:** It is used when you already give the dimensions to the part on the current view and you rotate the part and now come back to the previous view to get the existing dimensions. When you come to the actual view, dimension will automatically show.

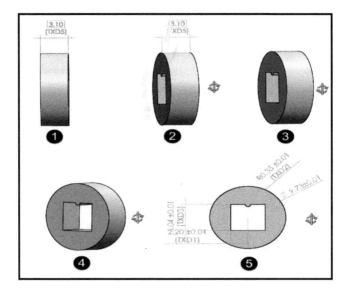

Figure 10 Dynamic annotation view

6. **View Orientation:** It is used to show any side of object like front view, top view, left view, right view, isolated view, and so on. and it is also used to set the multiple view of drawing area like you can create four view in one time in which you can show different side of view.

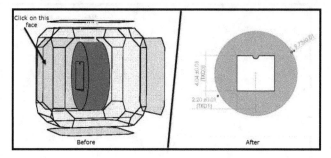

Figure 11 View orientation

7. **Display style:** It is a visual style which is used to set the visual style of design like wireframe, shaded, realistic, and so on.

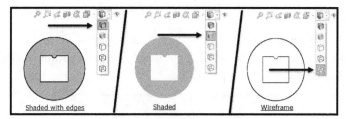

Figure 12 Display style

8. **Hide all type:** It is used to create the supporting element of design; it is used to hide or unhide them like plane, axis, origin, and so on.

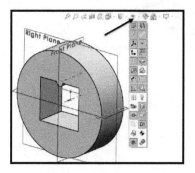

Figure 13 Hide all type

9. **Edit appearance:** It is used to edit the appearance of material editing or material apply. If you want to edit, first click on edit appearance then select appearance, after that, select material type then by going to the editing tab, the material can be edited.

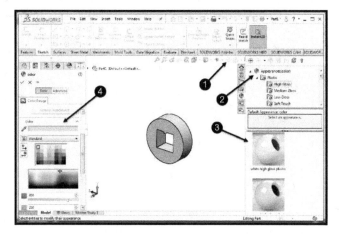

Figure 14 Edit appearance

10. **Apply scene**: It is used to change the background of page. It is used to set the background like environment, any simple scene or light scene, and so on.

Figure 15 Apply scene

11. **View setting:** It is used to give a real view to the design of object like perspective view or shadow, and so on.

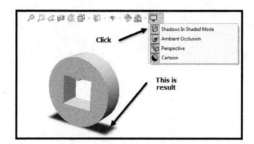

Figure 16 View setting

CHAPTER 2
Sketch

How to Start Sketch with Plane?

There are two types of sketches one is 2D and second is 3D. For 2D plan, firstly select the plan and then click on sketch. If you want 3D sketch, then you can directly click on sketch, there is no need to select any plan because 3D sketch works on three axis at the same time.

Step 1: First of all, select the plane which you want. I am selecting **Front Plane**.

Figure 17 Select plane

Step 2: **Ribbon**: Sketch tab ➤ Sketch.

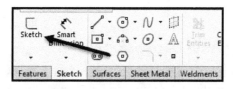

Figure 18 click sketch

Step 3: Now click on the rectangle tool for creating a rectangle.

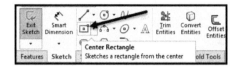

Figure 19 Click rectangle tool

Step 4: Click on center rectangle. I want to create center rectangle.

Figure 20 Select rectangle type

Step 5: Pick center point and then pick the corner point.

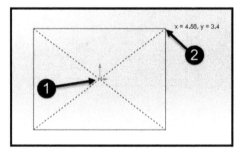

Figure 21 Create rectangle

How to use Smart Dimension?

Smart dimension is used to change or show the dimension of any object. It is used for linear, aligned, radius, and diameter.

Step 1: **Ribbon**: Sketch tab ➤ Smart dimension.

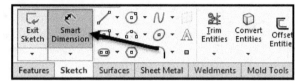

Figure 22 click smart dimension tool

Step 2: Pick on line.

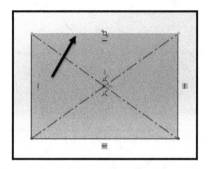

Figure 23 pick on line

Step 3: Pick on free space for dimension then specify dimension and click on **Finish**.

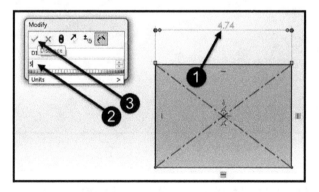

Figure 24 Show dimension

Line

There are three types of line. You can select line according to your need.

Step 1: First of all, select any plane then click on **Sketch**.

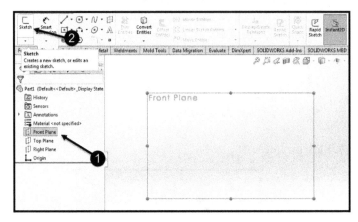

Figure 25 Start sketch

Step 2: Create a line. There are three types of line.

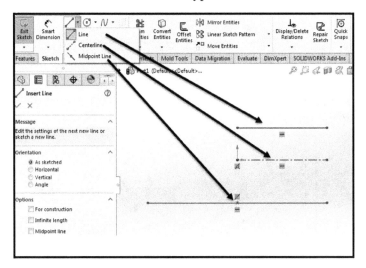

Figure 26 Line type

Note: There are many types of methods of creating line and different use of lines. Whenever you want that particular line, you can select that line type.

1. **As sketched:** It is used to create a free hand line in your sketch as you want to create.

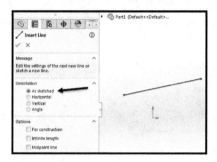

Figure 27 Simple line

2. **Horizontal line: Horizontal** is used to create a horizontal line. To create this line, you need to pick first point and second point only.

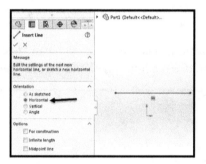

Figure 28 Horizontal line option

3. **Vertical line: Vertical** is used to create vertical linear line only. To create this line pick first point and then second point.

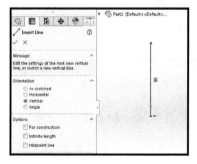

Figure 29 Vertical line option

4. **Angle line: Angle** is used to create tilt line whose angle is also given. To create this line firstly, select angle option and after that distance and give angel to that then pick a point.

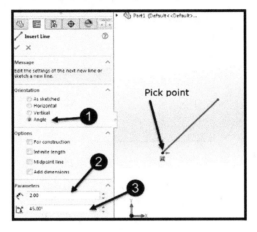

Figure 30 Angle line option

5. **For construction:** It is used when you want to create a reference line. It can also be used in horizontal and vertical angle.

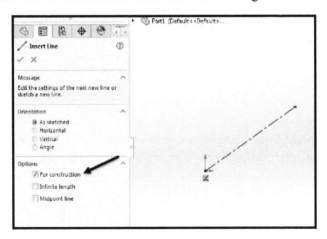

Figure 31 Construction line option

6. **Infinite length:** It is used to create infinite line which has no length.

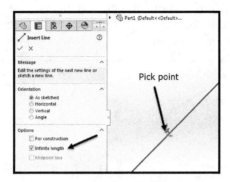

Figure 32 Infinite length line option

7. **Midpoint line:** It is used to create a line from center point and it is equal from both sides.

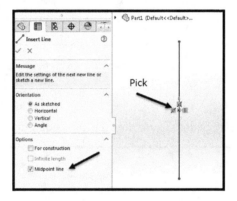

Figure 33 Midpoint line option

Rectangle

It has five types:

1. **Corner rectangle**: To create this rectangle, pick its first corner and then pick its opposite corner.

2. **Center rectangle**: To create this rectangle, pick its center point and then pick its corner point.

3. **3-point corner rectangle**: To create this rectangle pick its first point then pick its second linear point and same as that, pick third point.

4. **3point center rectangle**: To create three point rectangle, firstly you need to select the center point then pick the midpoint of line and then pic the corner point of rectangle.

5. **Parallelogram**: Parallelogram rectangle is same as three point rectangle. But there is a small difference between both of them that you can create third point tilt.

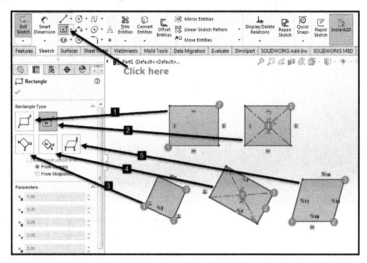

Figure 34 Rectangle types

Slot

It is used to create a slot. There are four types of slot.

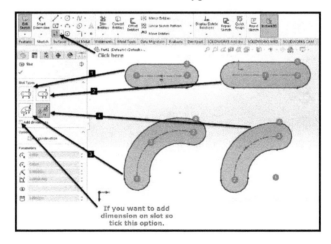

Figure 35 Slot types

Circle

You can create a circle by two methods. For the first circle there should be a center and for next circle there should be edge so that you can create edge.

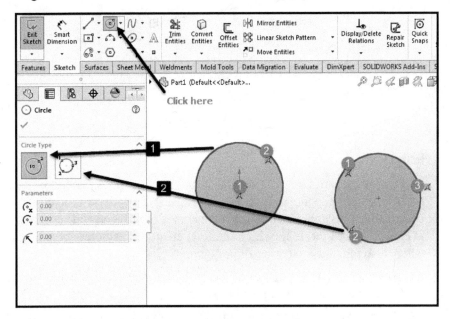

Figure 36 Circle types

Arc

Arc can be created by three methods. It is a part of circle.

1. **Center point arc:** To create this arc, you have to pick center point of arc then pick its starting and end point.

2. **Tangent arc:** First pick the end point of the object on which you want to create an arc and then pick the end point of arc.

3. **3point arc:** To create this arc pick starting and end point of arc and then pic the second point of arc which is actually the top point of arc.

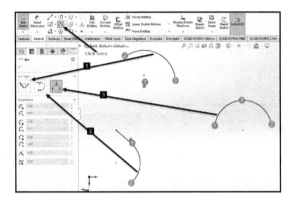

Figure 37 Arc types

Polygon

Polygon is created from radius and it has 3 to 40 sides. There are two types of polygon, one is Inscribed circle in which there is a circle in between the polygon which touches the corner of polygon and second one is circumscribed circle in which circle is created outside of the polygon which also touches the corner of polygon.

1. **Inscribed circle polygon:** This polygon is created outside of the circle but touch the edges of the circle.

2. **Circumscribed circle polygon:** This polygon is created outside of the circle but it touches the edges of circle.

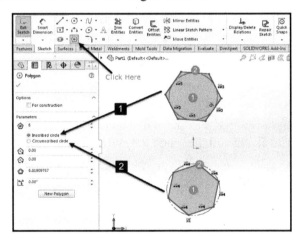

Figure 38 Polygon types

Spline

Spline means special line. There are four type of spline in SolidWorks.

1. Spline can be created by clicking point to point.

2. In style spline, you can control spline by its point.

3. Use this option to create a spline above the surface. Equation driven curve spline works according to its spline equation.

Ellipse

Ellipse is a type of circle which is created on two axis in which one axis is major axis and other one is minor. There are four types of ellipse in SolidWorks.

1. Ellipse

2. Partial ellipse

3. Parabola

4. Conic

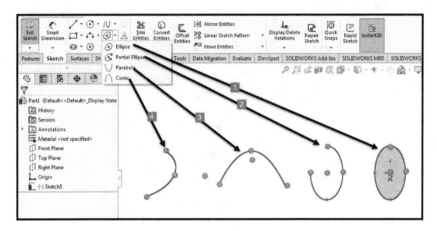

Figure 39 Ellipse types

Fillet

Fillet is used to convert the corner shape into curve. This curve can be set by radius.

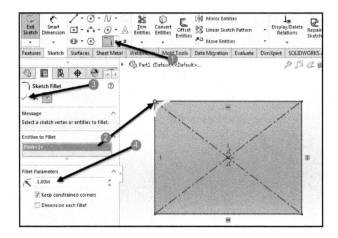

Figure 40 Fillet use

Chamfer

Chamfer is used to cut the corner shape. This cut can be set by two types.

1. Angle-distance
2. Distance to distance

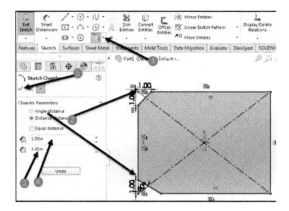

Figure 41 Chamfer use

3D Plane

3D plane is used to create a plane of 3D sketch, it work as a reference plane on 3D sketch.

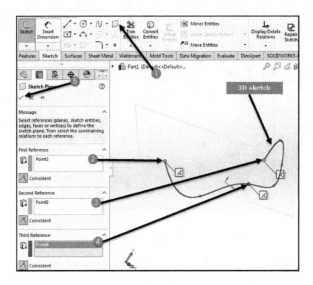

Figure 42 3D plane

Text

Text is used to print the text on any object it can be converted into 3D text.

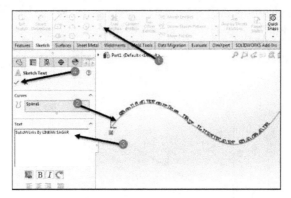

Figure 43 Text with curve path

Point

Point is used as a reference. Point is used as a reference or vertex in any sketch.

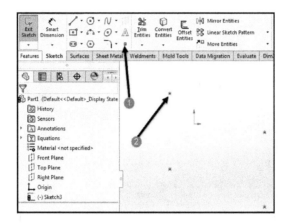

Figure 44 Point

Trim

Trim is used to remove the extra part of any sketch. Trim is used in the following five ways:

1. Power trim
2. Corner
3. Trim away inside
4. Trim away outside
5. Trim to closest

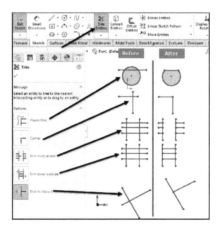

Figure 45 Trim types

Extend

Extend is used to extend line or arc on behalf of any target object.

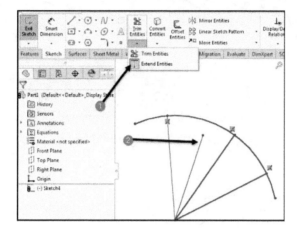

Figure 46 Extend

Convert Entities

Use convert entities to convert any close sketch or any edge to sketch.

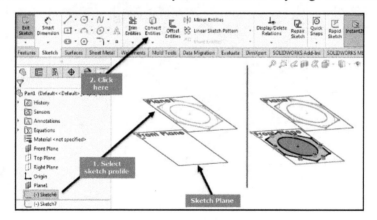

Figure 47 Convert entities

Intersection Curve

Intersection curve is used to create an intersection curve on part. For intersection curve there is a use of plane or surface.

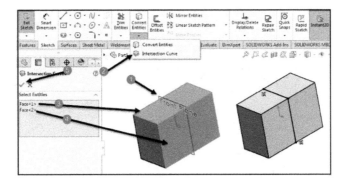

Figure 48 Intersection Curve

Offset

Offset is used to create the second and same object of sketch parallel to the first sketch.

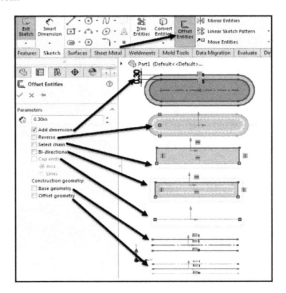

Figure 49 Offset types and option

Mirror

Mirror is used to create the opposite entities of any sketch. For mirror there should be at least one axis which can be taken as a reference for mirror.

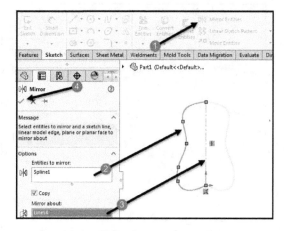

Figure 50 Mirror tool use

Linear Sketch Pattern

Linear sketch pattern is used to create multiple linear copies of any entities of sketch.

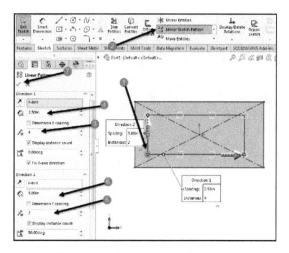

Figure 51 Linear sketch pattern

Circular Sketch Pattern

Circular sketch pattern is used to create circular copy of any entities of sketch.

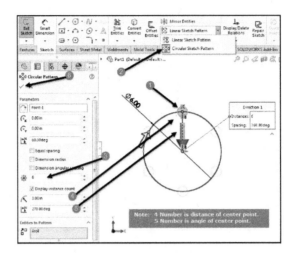

Figure 52 Circular sketch pattern

CHAPTER 3
Features

Extrude

Extrude is used to increase the height of any sketch so that you can convert it into the 3D object. Extrude converts the sketch into the body.

Step 1: First of all, select **Front Plane** and click on **Sketch**.

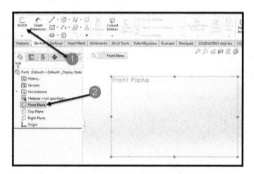

Figure 53 Start sketch

Step 2: After that create a sketch. Then click on **Exit Sketch** for close sketch.

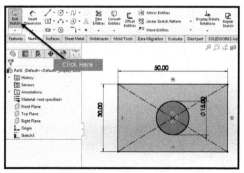

Figure 54 Create a rectangle and circle

Step 3: Select sketch profile. And click on **Extrude**.

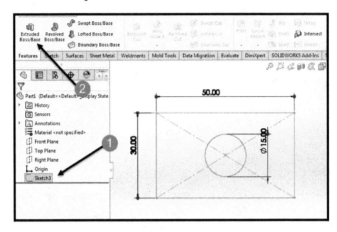

Figure 55 Click extrude tool

Step 4: Specify height for extrude and then click on finish mode.

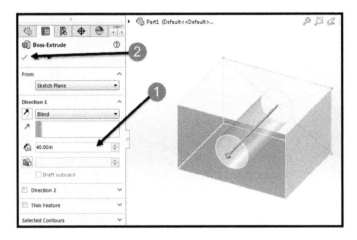

Figure 56 Specify distance

Note: There are many options while using extrude which has many uses and you can use according to your need. Details are given as follows:

1. **From:** When you want to extrude. And to change the position of extrude. Use the **From** option in that place.

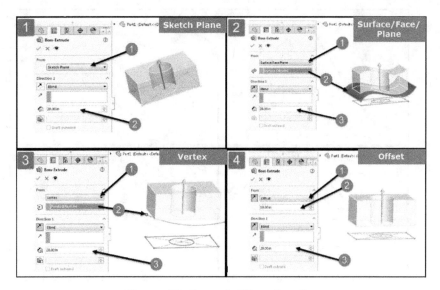

Figure 57 Extrude "from" option

2. **Direction1:** It is used to decide the height of object which you want to extrude.

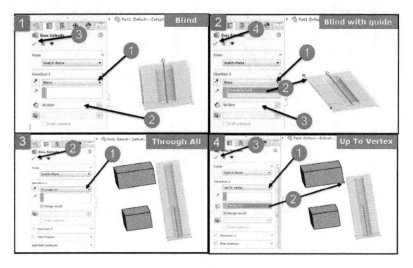

Figure 58 Extrude "direction" option-1

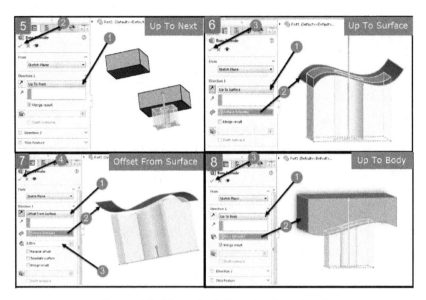

Figure 59 Extrude "direction" option-2

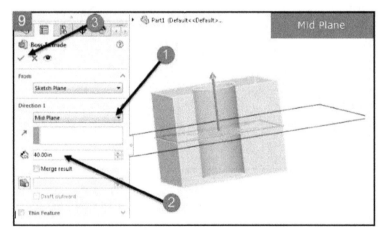

Figure 60 Extrude "direction" option-3

3. **Merge option:** Merge option is used to merge two bodies when extrude.

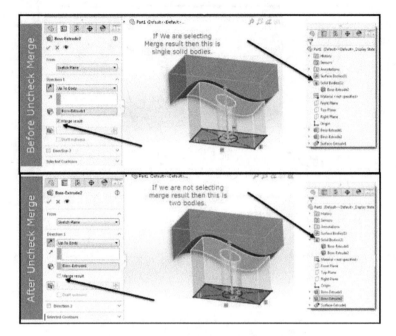

Figure 61 Merge option

4. **Draft angle:** It is used to extrude the object with the angle.

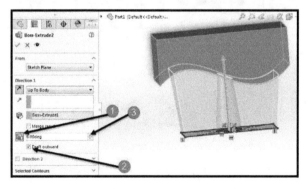

Figure 62 Draft angle

5. **Direction2:** It is used when you want to extrude an object from two sides, after selecting the direction2, the other side is automatically extrude. There is same option available as in **Direction1**.

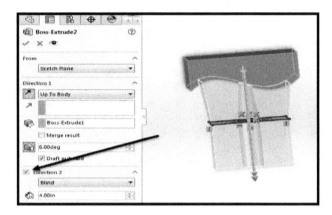

Figure 63 Direction 2 use

6. **Thin features:** Use **Thin features** to make solid body as Holo solid body.

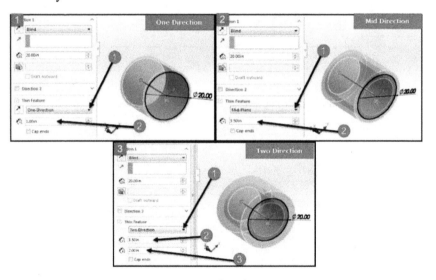

Figure 64 Thin features

Note: Reverse direction is used to change the side of direction.

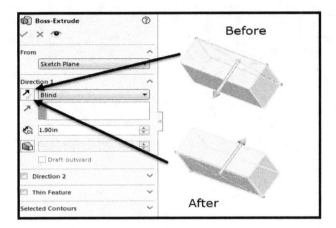

Figure 65 Reverse direction

Revolved

Revolve is used to create an object circular about any axis. To use revolve sketch should be closed and there should be at least one axis.

Step 1: First, select **Front Plane** and click on **Sketch**.

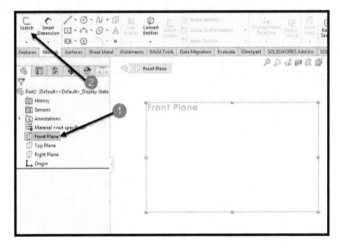

Figure 66 Start sketch

Step 2: After that, create a sketch with a reference axis. Then click on exit sketch for close sketch.

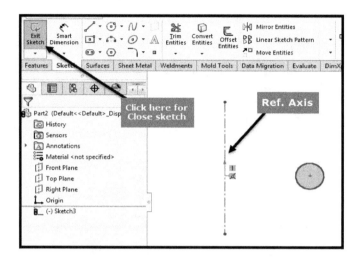

Figure 67 Create sketch for revolve

Step 3: Select **Sketch** profile and click on **Revolved** tool.

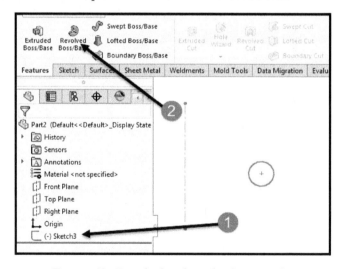

Figure 68 Finish sketch and select revolve

Step 4: Select axis and specify angle for revolve. Then click on **Finish**.

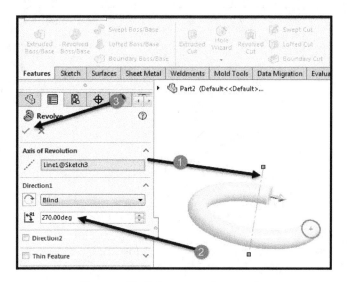

Figure 69 Select axis for revolve

Direction1: It is used to change the end shape or angle of revolve object at time of revolving it.

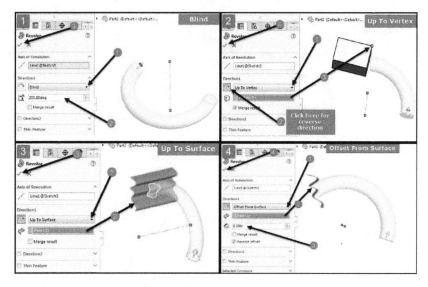

Figure 70 Revolve option-1

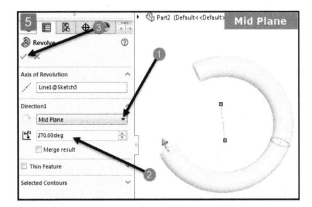

Figure 71 Revolve option-2

Direction2: If you've Revolved into a direction. And on the other side also have to revolve. Then use the direction 2.

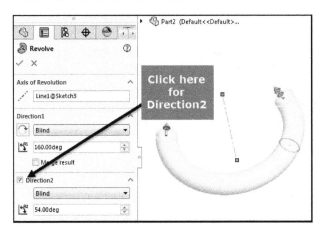

Figure 72 Direction-2

Thin Features: It is used to make a hole in the object. As if you want to make a hole in object you can use thin feature. You can give the thickness of object by three methods.

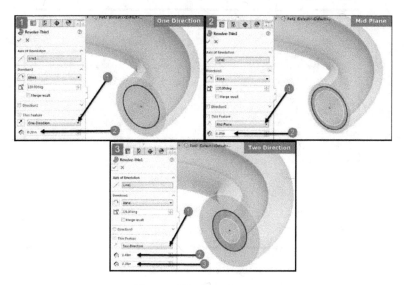

Figure 73 Thin features

Swept

In sweep command you can convert a path into any profile shape with the help of any profile. By following the profile, path shape can be converted.

Step 1: First, select **Front Plane** and click on **Sketch**.

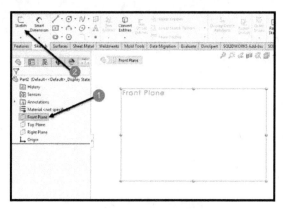

Figure 74 Start sketch

Step 2: After that create a sketch of path, like a Spline. Then click on **Exit Sketch** for closing the sketch.

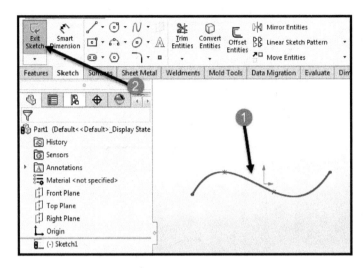

Figure 75 Create a path

Step 3: Select sketch and click on Reference plane.

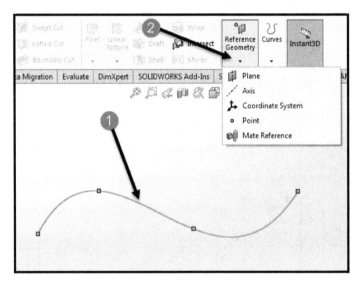

Figure 76 Create a plane

Step 4: Pick point and click on **Finish**.

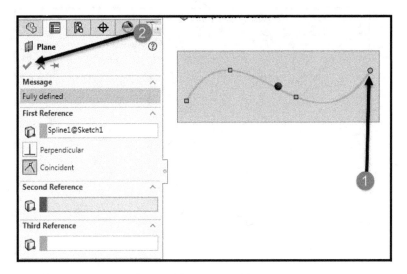

Figure 77 Select reference for plane

Step 5: Select **Plane** and click on **Sketch**.

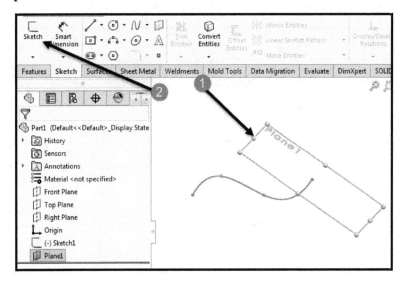

Figure 78 Start second sketch

Step 6: Create a sketch of profile, like a circle. Then click on **Exit Sketch** for closing the sketch.

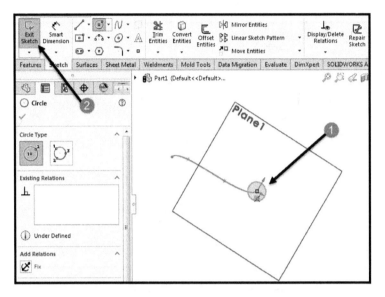

Figure 79 Create profile

Step 7: Select profile (circle) and click on **Swept** tool.

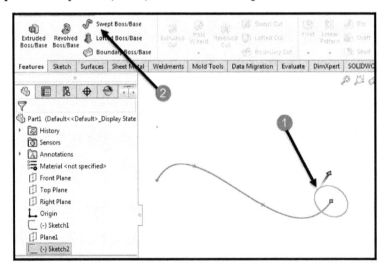

Figure 80 Click on swept

Step 8: Select path (Spline) and click on **Finish**.

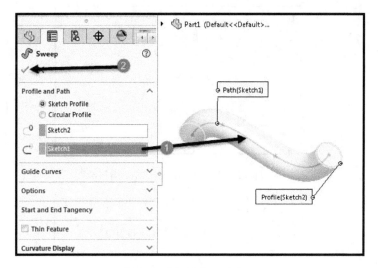

Figure 81 Select spline

Guide Curves: It helps to give the direction or shape of path.

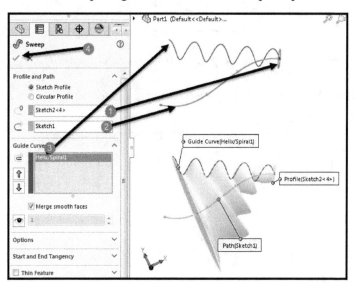

Figure 82 Guide curves option

Option: It is used for profile orientation and for twisting the path.

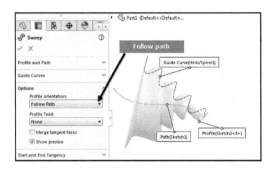

Figure 83 Follow path option

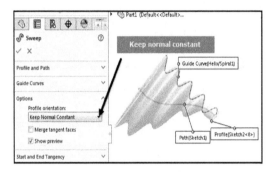

Figure 84 Keep normal constant option

Option – Profile twist: To give twist direction to Sweep's path, the profile uses the twist option.

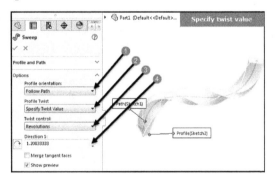

Figure 85 Profile twist option

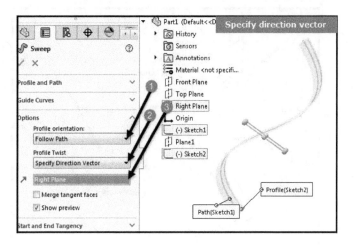

Figure 86 Specify direction vector

Step 1: First, create a spline of 3D sketch and create a line of 2D sketch.

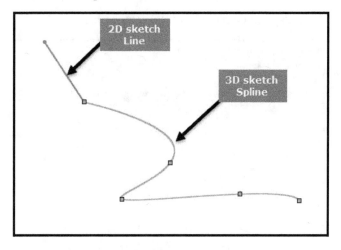

Figure 87 Create a 3D sketch

Step 2: Then select spline and click on surface extrude and give height.

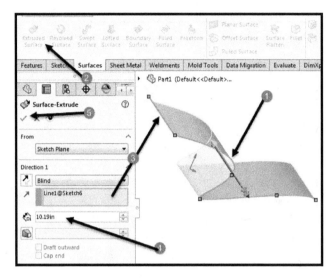

Figure 88 Surface extrude

Step 3: Select spline then click on Reference plane.

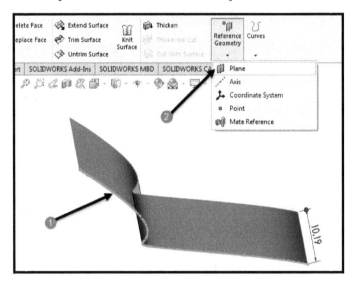

Figure 89 Plane

Step 4: Pick end point of spline and click on **Finish**.

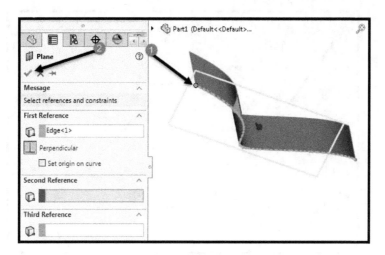

Figure 90 Plane ref.

Step 5: Select new plane and click on **Sketch**.

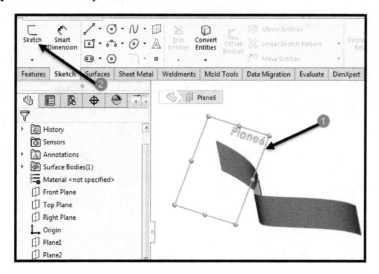

Figure 91 Start sketch

Step 6: Create a rectangle for profile and click on **Exit Sketch**.

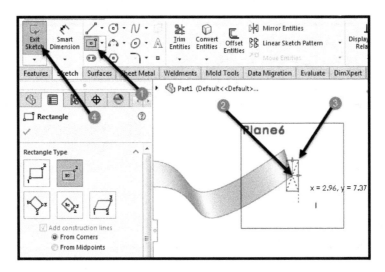

Figure 92 Create rectangle

Step 7: Use sweep tool and select **Minimum Twist**.

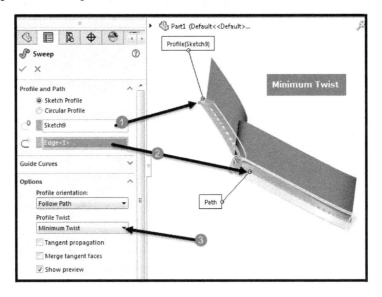

Figure 93 Minimum twist option

OR

Use sweep tool and select tangent to adjacent faces.

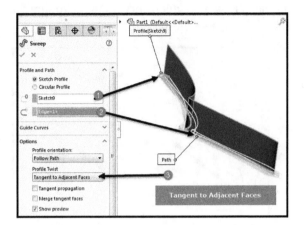

Figure 94 Tangent to adjacent faces

Start and end tangency: Start and end point is used to make tangent of the start and end point of the path.

Loft

It is used to convert two or more objects into the solid body but in same shape. You can also give the direction with the help of guide curve.

Step 1: First, create first sketch on front plane and create second sketch on another pallor plane of front plane.

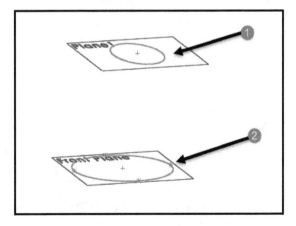

Figure 95 Create two different sketch

Step 2: After that, create two guide curves but make sure that there are two different sketches. Not a single sketch.

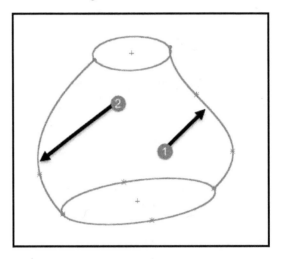

Figure 96 Create two different guide curves

Step 3: First, click on loft tool. Then select first profile sketch and select second profile sketch.

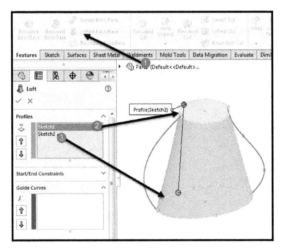

Figure 97 Loft tool use

Step 4: Select first guide curve and second guide curve. Then click on **Finish**.

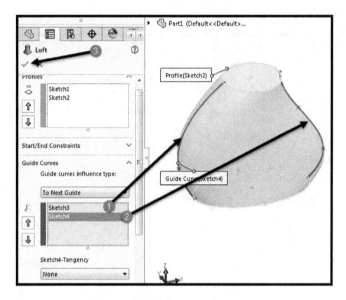

Figure 98 Select guide curves

Start/End constraints: To change the profile's direction and change the shape of the loft, use Start / End constraints.

1. Select the **None** option.

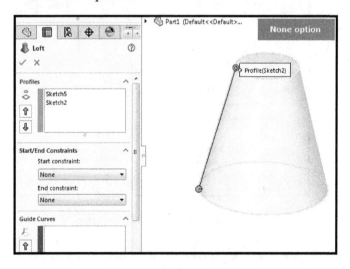

Figure 99 Start/End constraints

2. Direction vector

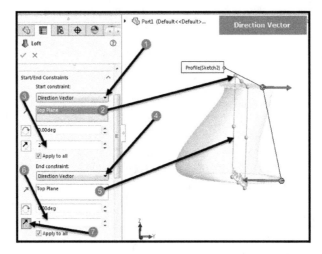

Figure 100 Direction vector

3. Select the **Normal to profile** option.

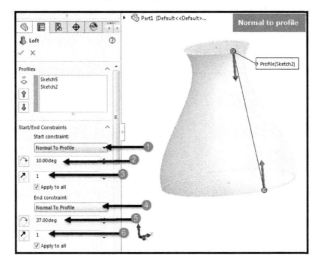

Figure 101 Normal to profile

Centerline parameters: To guide curve from Centerline, use the centerline guide curve.

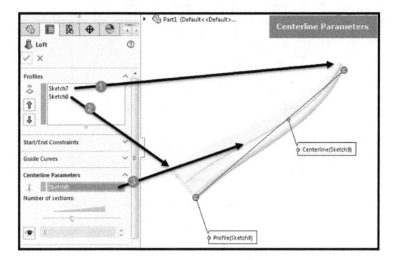

Figure 102 Centerline parameters

Marge tangent faces: To merge the tangent face in the Loft tool, use the merge tangent face option.

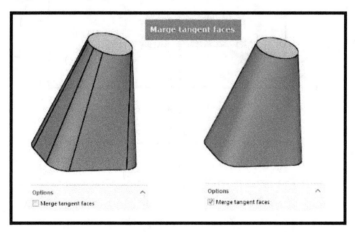

Figure 103 Merge tangent faces

Close loft: Use the closed loft to complete the incomplete loft. When two sketches are on the same plane and on a sketch perpendicular plane then it requires three sketches.

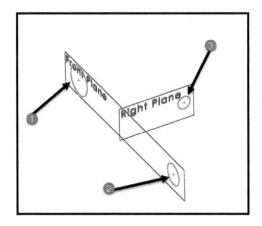

Figure 104 Create three sketches

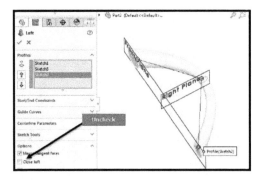

Figure 105 Uncheck close loft

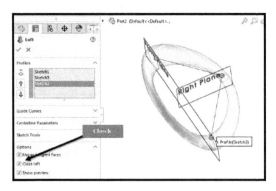

Figure 106 Check close loft

Boundary

Boundary tool is like a little loft. But even if there is a profile in the boundary tool, you can use the boundary tool.

Step 1: First, create three different sketches.

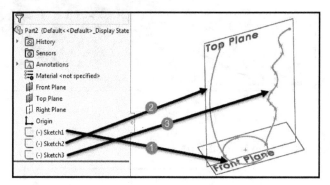

Figure 107 Create three sketches

Step 2: After that, click on loft and select sketches and then finish.

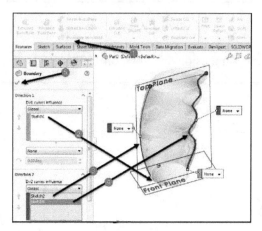

Figure 108 Boundary tool use

Extruded Cut

Extruded cut is used to cut the solid object.

Step 1: First, select sketch profile.

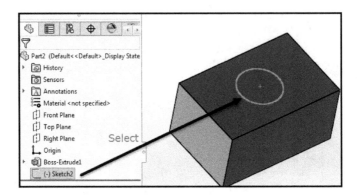

Figure 109 Select circle

Step 2: Click on **Extruded Cut** tool.

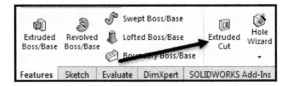

Figure 110 extrude cut tool

Step 3: Specify dimension and click on **Finish** mode.

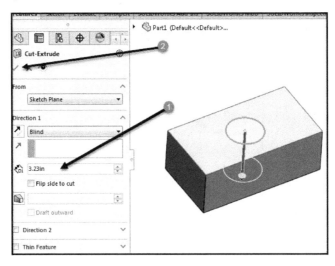

Figure 111 Cut dimension

Hole Wizard

Use of the Whole Wizard Tool is done to cut the hole of the screw shape.

Step 1: First, click on hole wizard tool.

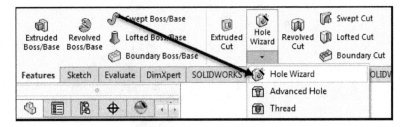

Figure 112 Click hole wizard

Step 2: First, click on **Positions** tab and then click on **3D Sketch** button.

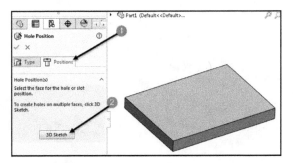

Figure 113 Click 3D Sketch button

Step 3: Specify position on solid face.

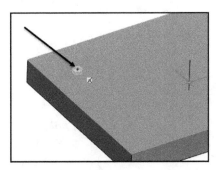

Figure 114 Specify position

Step 4: Click on **Smart Dimension** then pick center point of hole wizard and edge. Then specify dimension.

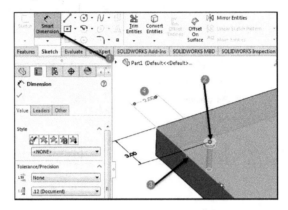

Figure 115 Use smart dimension

Step 5: Click on hole type tab then select hole type and standard.

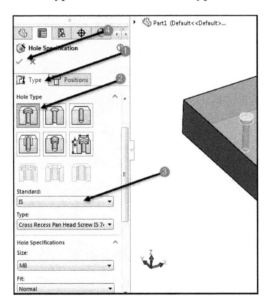

Figure 116 Select hole type

Thread

Thread tool is used to cut the thread of the screw.

Step 1: First, click on thread tool.

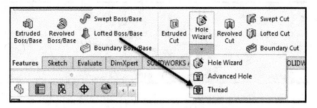

Figure 117 Thread tool

Step 2: Select circular edge then set thread setting.

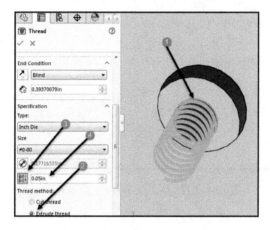

Figure 118 Thread setting

Revolved Cut

Revolved cut tool is used to cut into circular shape. There is a close sketch and an axis for revolved cut.

Step 1: First, create a sketch and axis.

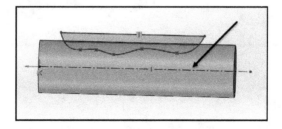

Figure 119 Create a sketch

Step 2: Select sketch profile then click on **Revolved Cut**.

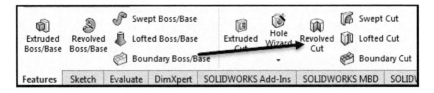

Figure 120 Select revolved cut tool

Step 3: Select axis then specify angle.

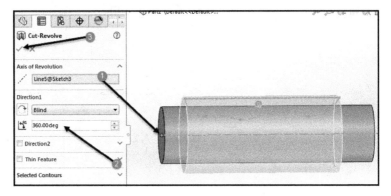

Figure 121 Select axis and specify angle

After that.

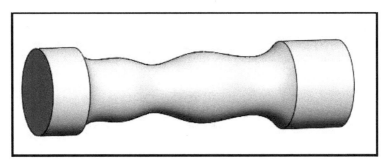

Figure 122 After use

Swept Cut

To cut through paths and profiles, use the swept cut tool.

Step 1: First, create a path and profile.

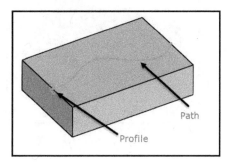

Figure 123 Profile and path

Step 2: Click on **Swept Cut**.

Figure 124 Swept cut tool

Step 3: First select profile then select path.

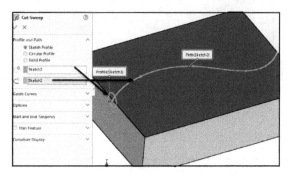

Figure 125 Select profile and path

Step 4: After selecting profile and path, click on the Finish mode.

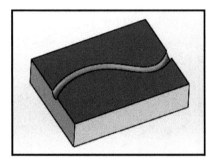

Figure 126 After

Loft Cut

Loft cut is like Loft Tool. But instead of creating a solid object, it is done to cut the shape. There are different options to cut in the loft cut as in the loft.

Step 1: First, create two profile and one guide curve.

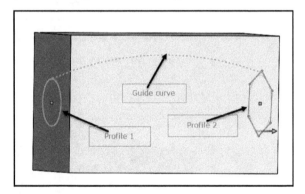

Figure 127 Create three sketches

Step 2: After that click on loft tool.

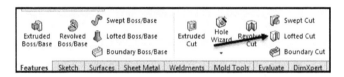

Figure 128 Loft cut tool

Step 3: Select profile and guide curve then click on finish tick.

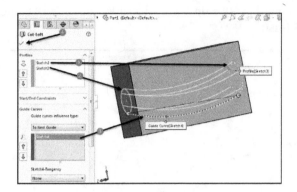

Figure 129 Loft cut use

Boundary Cut

Use the boundary cut tool to remove part of the solid body.

Step 1: First, create one profile and two guide curves.

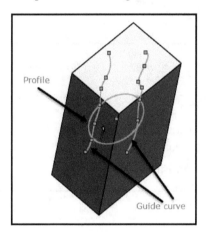

Figure 130 Create three sketches

Step 2: Click on **Boundary Cut** tool.

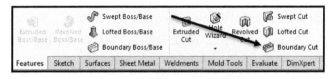

Figure 131 Boundary cut tool

Step 3: Select first profile then select two guide curves one by one and click on **Finish**.

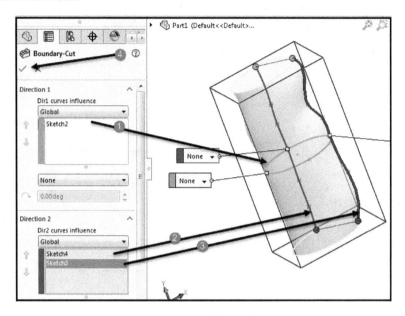

Figure 132 Use boundary cut

Fillet

Use the fillet tool to curve the edge. Radius is necessary for this. There are many types of fillet tools.

Step 1: First, click on **Fillet** tool.

Figure 133 Fillet

Step 2: Select edge and then specify radius.

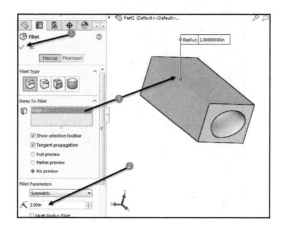

Figure 134 Select edge

Step 3: Click on **Finish** tick.

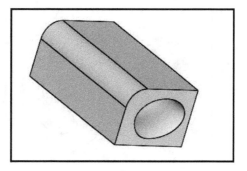

Figure 135 After use

Chamfer

In the solid body, use the chamfer tool to cut the tilt in the edges. The chamfer can be used in two ways where first is distance and second is angle.

Step 1: First, click on chamfer tool.

Figure 136 Chamfer

Step 2: Select the edge then specify distance.

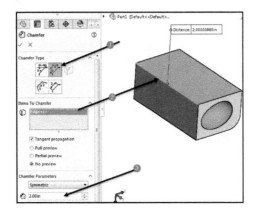

Figure 137 Select edge

Step 3: Click finish tick.

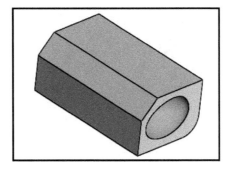

Figure 138 After use

Linear Pattern

The linear pattern is used to copy the solid part to the linear multiple. It is used to copy multiple objects together in two directions.

Step 1: First, click on **Linear Pattern** tool.

Figure 139 Linear pattern

Step 2: Click on features then select **Solid part**.

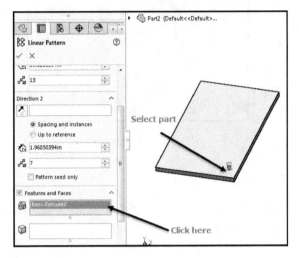

Figure 140 Select solid part

Step 3: Select edge then specify distance and specify number.

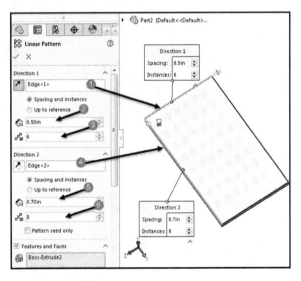

Figure 141 Specify distance and specify number

Step 4: After using the linear pattern.

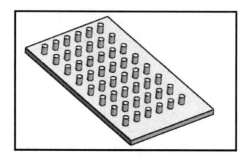

Figure 142 After that

Circular Pattern

Use circular pattern tool to copy circular multiply to solid part.

Step 1: First, click on **Circular Pattern** tool.

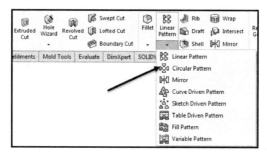

Figure 143 Circular pattern

Step 2: Click on **Features** and select solid part.

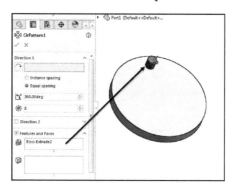

Figure 144 Select solid part

Step 3: Select circular edge or circular face then specify number.

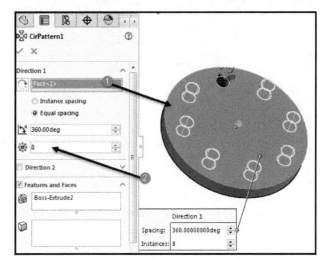

Figure 145 Select circular edge or circular face

Curve Driven Pattern

Use the curve driven pattern to multiple copy the solid part on the path.

Step 1: First, create a curve and solid part.

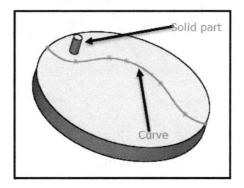

Figure 146 Create a curve and solid part

Step 2: Click on **Curve Driven Pattern** tool.

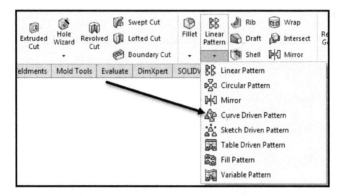

Figure 147 Curve driven pattern tool

Step 3: Select curve and solid part then specify number and distance.

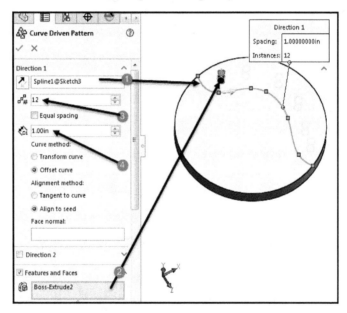

Figure 148 Specify number and distance

Sketch Driven Pattern

Use the curve driven pattern to multiple copy the solid part on the point.

Step 1: First, make some points.

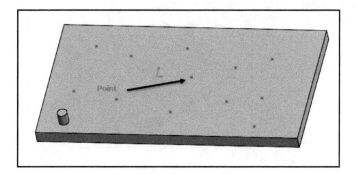

Figure 149 Make some points

Step 2: Click on **Sketch Driven Pattern**.

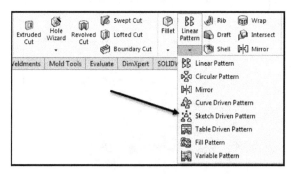

Figure 150 Sketch driven pattern

Step 3: First, select the sketch with the point then select solid part profile.

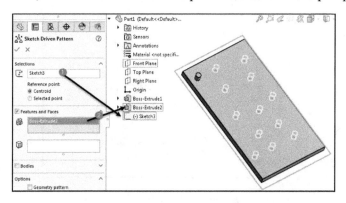

Figure 151 select solid part profile

Step 3: After that click on finish mode.

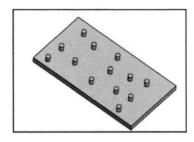

Figure 152 After that

Rib

Creates a thin wall to support two faces, for which Rib uses the tool.

Step 1: First, click on **Plane** tool.

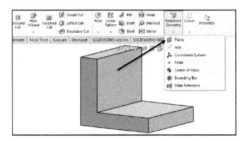

Figure 153 Plane tool

Step 2: Select first face.

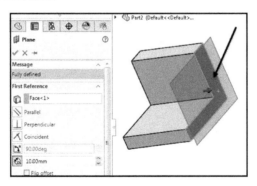

Figure 154 Select first face

Step 3: Select second face then click on **Finish**.

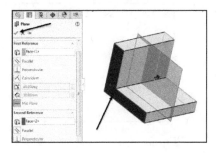

Figure 155 Select second face

Step 4: Select the plane and click on **Sketch** tool.

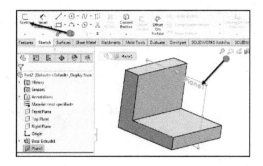

Figure 156 Click on sketch tool

Step 5: Create a line and finish sketch.

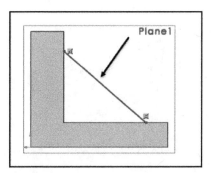

Figure 157 Create a line

Step 6: Select line and click on **Rib** tool.

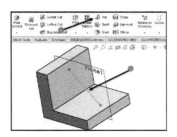

Figure 158 Click on rib tool

Step 7: Specify rib thickness and click on **Finish**.

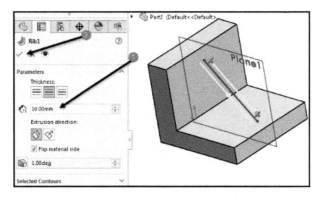

Figure 159 Specify rib thickness

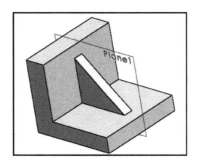

Figure 160 After that

Shell

Shell tool is used to convert solid body to thin outer wall.

Step 1: First, click on **Shell** tool.

Figure 161 Click on Shell tool

Step 2: Select the face which you want to remove.

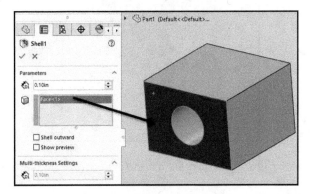

Figure 162 Select that face

Step 3: Specify thickness and click on finish option.

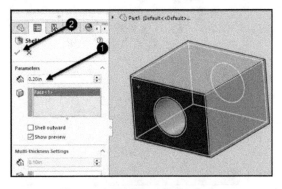

Figure 163 Specify thickness

Wrap

The wrap feature in SolidWorks is good if you are trying to project a sketch without any distortion around a surface and cut or add material to that part.

Step 1: Create a solid object and a sketch as it is given below, in two different planes.

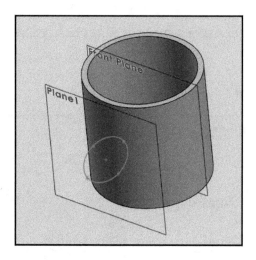

Figure 164 Create a solid object and a sketch

Step 2: Select sketch then click on **Wrap** tool.

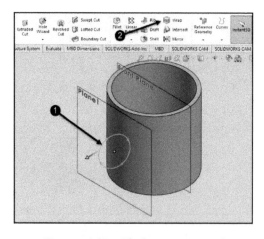

Figure 165 Click on wrap tool

Step 3: Select emboss option of wrap type and select face of solid part. Then specify thickness and click on finish mode.

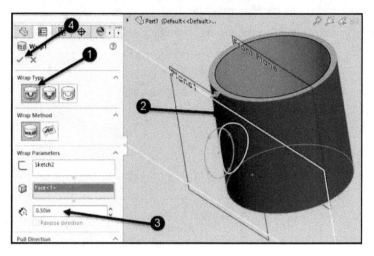

Figure 166 Select emboss

Note: Types of wrap

1. Emboss
2. Deboss
3. Scribe

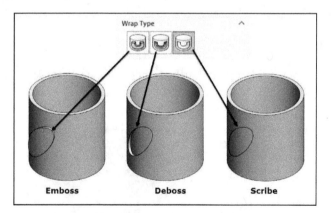

Figure 167 Types of wrap

Intersect

Select all the surface bodies. As you select each one, they populate the Selections box in the PropertyManager.

Step 1: Create a solid object and a surface extrude, as it is given below.

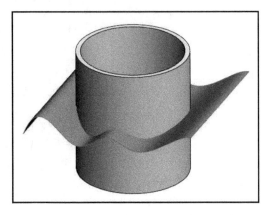

Figure 168 Create a solid object and a Surface extrude

Step 2: Click on **Intersect** tool.

Figure 169 Intersect

Step 3: Select solid part and surface then click on **Intersect** button.

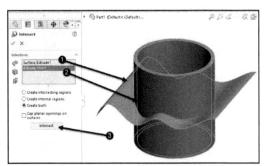

Figure 170 Select solid part and surface

Step 4: Tick on **Region 1** then click on finish mode.

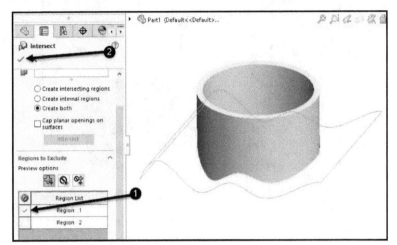

Figure 171 Tick on region 1

Mirror

Use the mirror tool to copy the reverse part of a plane through a plane. Select a face or plane to mirror about then click on **Insert | Mirror Part**. See Creating Opposite-Hand Versions of Parts. Assembly Mirror an assembly feature. In an assembly, click on **Assembly Features (Assembly** tab on the Command Manager) and click on **Mirror,** or click on **Insert | Assembly Feature | Mirror**.

Step 1: Click on **Mirror** tool.

Figure 172 Click on mirror tool

Step 2: Pick bodies option and select body then pick face/plane option and select face.

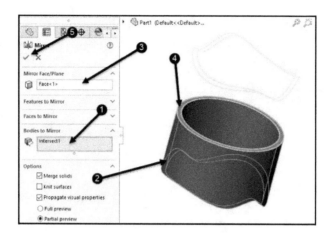

Figure 173 Mirror tool use

Step 3: After that click on **Finish Mode** option.

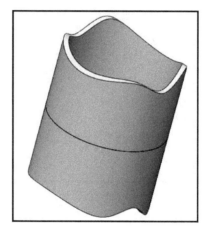

Figure 174 Finish mode

Dome

Use the dome tool to make a curve shape above the face. To create a dome:
Click on **Dome** option in the **Features** toolbar or click **Insert | Features | Dome**.

Step 1: Click on **Dome** tool.

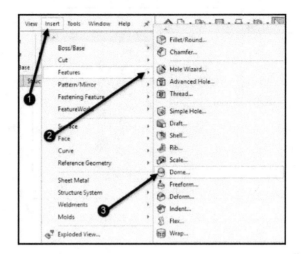

Figure 175 Dome tool

Step 2: Select face of cylinder body and specify distance.

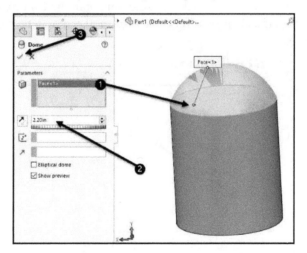

Figure 176 Cylinder body

Step 3: Then click on finish mode.

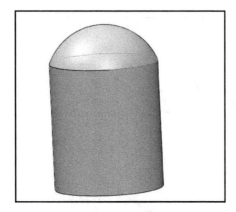

Figure 177 After that

Freeform

Use the freeform tool to make a curve shape above the face. Navigate to **Insert | Features | Freeform** or click on the Freeform icon. Under Face settings select the **Face** to deform. Add curves in the Control Curves box. Add points in the Control Points box. Now you can drag the points to form the surface.

Step 1: Click on **Freeform** tool.

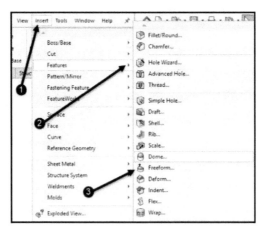

Figure 178 Freeform

Step 2: Select face and click on **Add Curves** option.

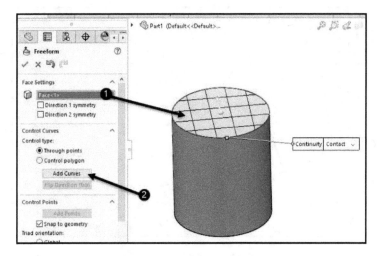

Figure 179 Add curves

Step 3: Pick axis on face and again click on **Add Curves** option for off curves option.

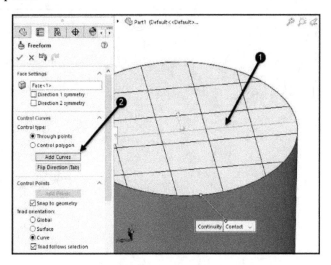

Figure 180 off curves option

Step 4: Click on **Add Points** option and pick point.

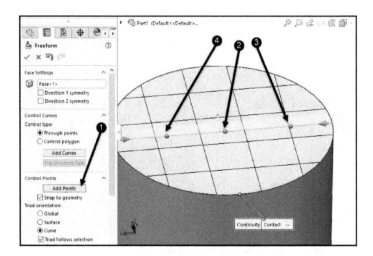

Figure 181 Add points

Step 5: Again click on **Add Points** option for off Add Points option and pick a point. Then specify y axis height.

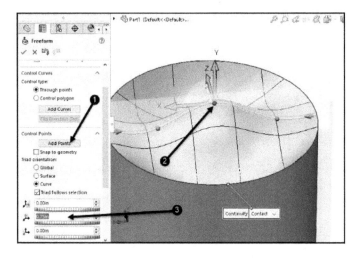

Figure 182 off "add points" option

Step 6: Then click on finish mode.

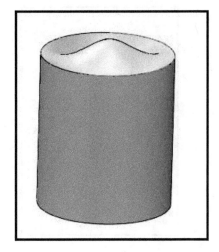

Figure 183 Then click on finish mode

Deform

Use the Deform Tool to convert solid body into any shape. To deform, it is also necessary to have a sketch, to convert the solid body into a shape.

Step 1: First, create a pipe shape and a reference line in another sketch.

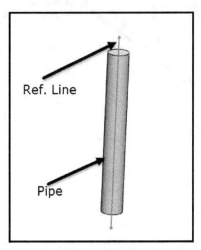

Figure 184 Create a pipe shape and a reference line

Step 2: Create a Spline for deform.

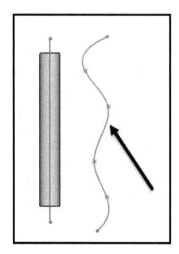

Figure 185 Create a Spline

Step 3: Click on the Deform tool.

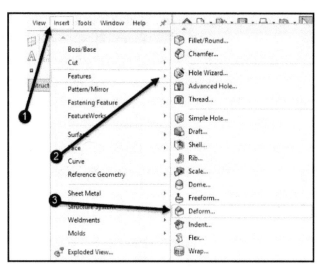

Figure 186 Deform tool

Step 4: Select initial curve and target curve.

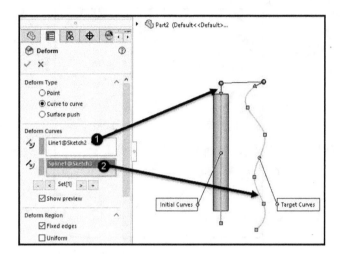

Figure 187 Select initial curve and target curve

Step 5: Select solid body and **Curve direction** option.

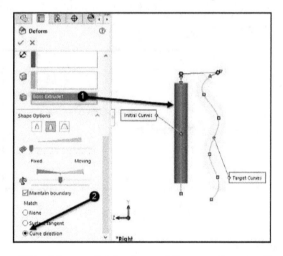

Figure 188 Select solid body and "curve direction" option

Step 6: Click on finish mode.

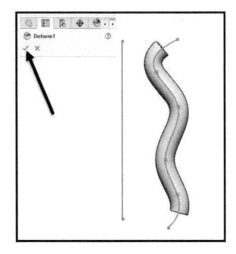

Figure 189 Click on finish mode

Flex

Flex features deform complex models in an intuitive manner.

Step 1: Create a simple rod. As given below.

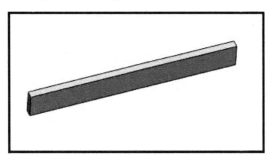

Figure 190 Create a simple rod

Step 2- Click on **Flex** tool.

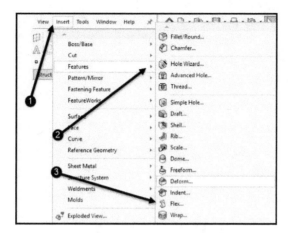

Figure 191 Flex tool

Step 3: Select rod and twisting option. Then specify angle for twisting.

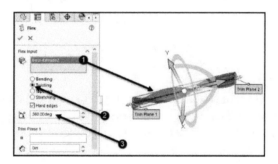

Figure 192 Specify angle

Step 4- Click on finish mode.

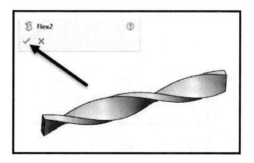

Figure 193 Click on finish mode

Note: Types of Flex

1. Bending
2. Twisting
3. Tapering
4. Stretching

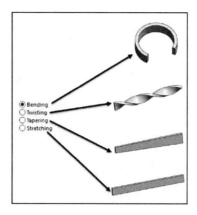

Figure 194 Types of Flex

Indent

Use of indent tool to cover any face using thickness and clearance values to create the feature. Depending on the body type selected (solid or surface), you specify the clearance between the target body and the tool body, and a thickness for the indent feature. The indent feature can deform or cut material from the target body.

Step 1: Create a Cylinder shape.

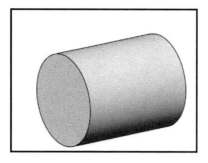

Figure 195 Create a Cylinder shape

Step 2: Then create a plate with extrude tool. But make sure the merge option is not checked as given below:

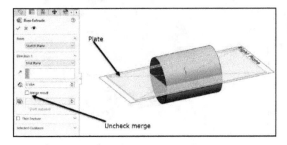

Figure 196 Create a plate with extrude tool

Step 3: Click on **Indent** tool.

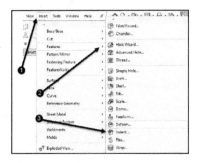

Figure 197 Click on Indent tool

Step 4: Select target body and tool body region.

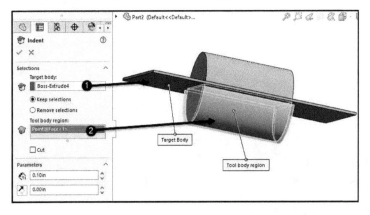

Figure 198 Tool body region

Step 5: Click on finish mode.

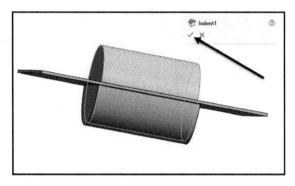

Figure 199 Finish mode

CHAPTER 4
Surface

Extruded Surface

Extrude surface is used to increase the height of any sketch so that you can convert it into the 3D object. Extrude surface converts the sketch into the surface body.

Step 1: Create a sketch.

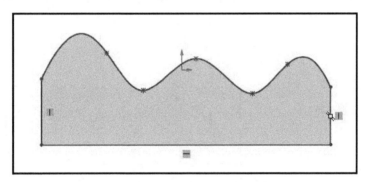

Figure 200 Create a sketch

Step 2: Click on **Extruded Surface**.

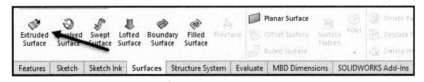

Figure 201 Extruded surface

Step 3: Specify the type of direction first and distance.

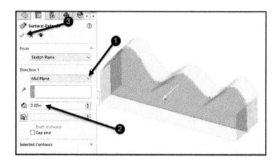

Figure 202 Direction first

Revolved surface

Revolve surface is used to create an object circular about any axis. To use revolve surface, sketch should be at least one axis.

Step 1: Create a line and convert construction line for reference line.

Figure 203 Create a line and convert construction

Step 2: Create a Spline as given below.

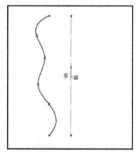

Figure 204 Create a Spline

Step 3: Select sketch and click on **Revolved Surface** tool.

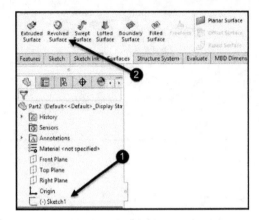

Figure 205 Revolved surface tool

Step 4: Specify angle and direction.

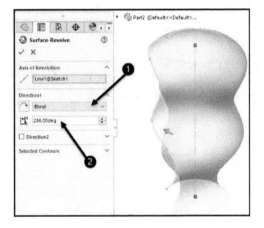

Figure 206 Specify angle

Swept surface

In swept surface command, you can convert a path into any profile shape with the help of any profile. By following the profile path shape can be converted. It is used to create hole shape.

Step 1: Create an arc. Then click on plane.

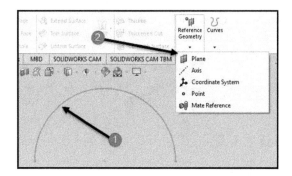

Figure 207 Click on plane

Step 2: Click on point of arc. Then click on finish.

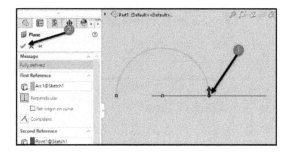

Figure 208 Point of arc

Step 3: Select plane and click on sketch.

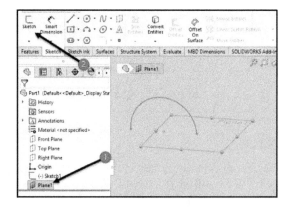

Figure 209 Click on sketch

Step 4: Again create an arc.

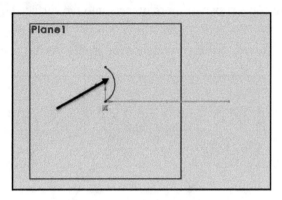

Figure 210 Again create an arc

Step 5: Click on **Swept Surface**.

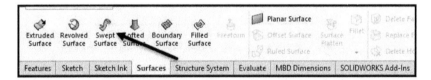

Figure 211 Swept surface

Step 6: Select profile and path. Then click on finish mode.

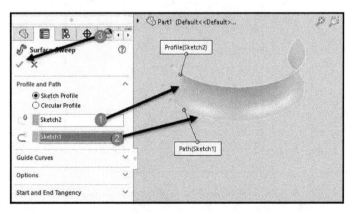

Figure 212 Select profile and path

Lofted Surface

It is used to convert two or more objects into the surface body but in same shape. You can also give the direction with the help of guide curve.

Step 1: Create two different sketches for profile. As has been given below.

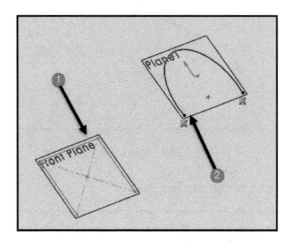

Figure 213 Create two different sketches for profile

Step 2: Select side plane. Then create an arc.

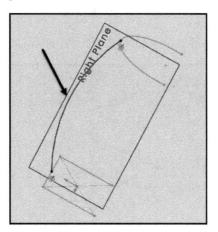

Figure 214 Select side plane

Step 3: Click on lofted surface.

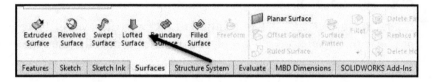

Figure 215 Lofted surface

Step 4: Select both profiles and guide curve.

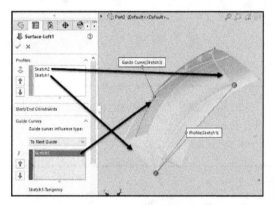

Figure 216 Select both profiles and guide curve

Step 5: Click on finish mode.

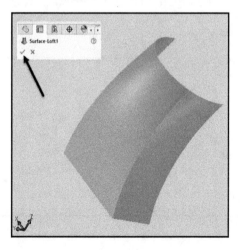

Figure 217 Finish mode

Boundary Surface

Boundary surface tool is like a little loft surface. But even if there is a profile in the boundary surface tool, you can use the boundary surface tool.

Step 1: Create two different sketches as given below.

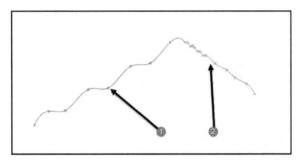

Figure 218 Create two different sketches

Step 2: Click on boundary surface.

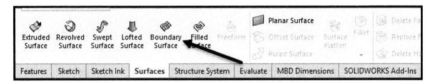

Figure 219 Boundary surface

Step 3: Select both sketches.

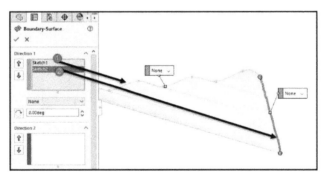

Figure 220 Select both sketches

Step 4: Click on finish mode.

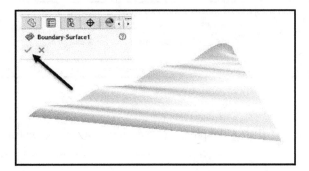

Figure 221 Finish mode

Filled Surface

To create a finished surface, you usually require an attached range. In it you can also give the guide curve.

Step 1: Create an ellipse.

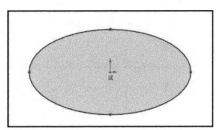

Figure 222 Create an ellipse

Step 2: After that create an arc in second sketch as given below.

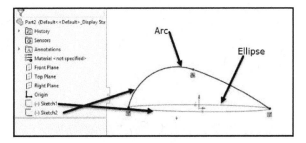

Figure 223 Create an arc in second sketch

Step 3: Click on filled surface.

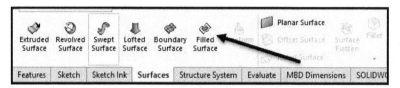

Figure 224 Click on filled surface

Step 4: Select ellipse for patch boundary and arc for constraint curves.

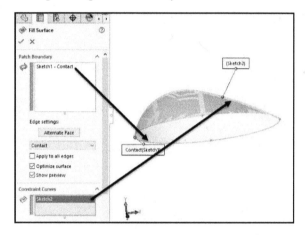

Figure 225 Select ellipse for patch boundary

Step 5: Click on finish mode.

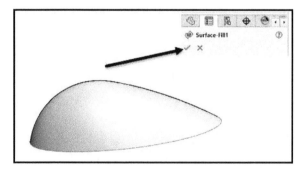

Figure 226 Click on finish mode

Planer Surface

Select the edge and use the planer surface tool to create a simple plane.

Step 1: Create an ellipse.

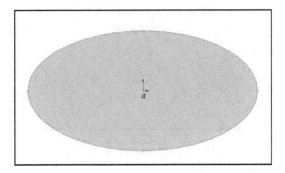

Figure 227 Create an ellipse

Step 2: Click on **Planer Surface** then select ellipse.

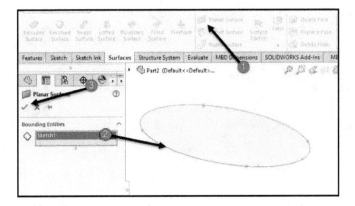

Figure 228 Click on planer surface

Offset Surface

Parallel to one surface uses offset surface tool to create second surface. Select surfaces or faces in the graphics area for Surface or Faces to Offset.

Step 1: Create a spline and use the extrude surface.

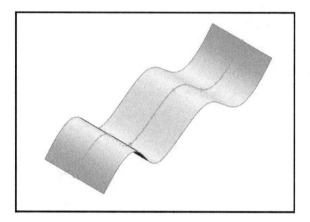

Figure 229 Create a spline

Step 2: Click on offset surface then select spline surface and specify a distance.

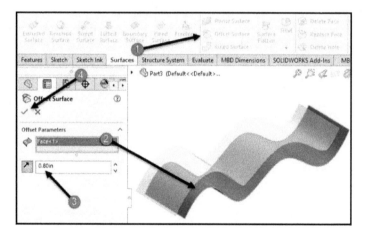

Figure 230 Click on offset surface

Ruled Surface

For many designs, creating solid geometry with features like boss extrude and cut will get the job done. But for more complicated shapes, it's impossible to build with solid modeling techniques alone. These more complicated geometries will certainly require surfacing techniques.

Although the shape might be complicated, the tools and techniques to produce it don't have to be.

Step 1: Create an arc and center line.

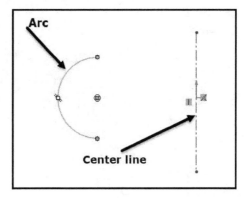

Figure 231 Create an arc and center line

Step 2: Click on revolved surface and specify angle.

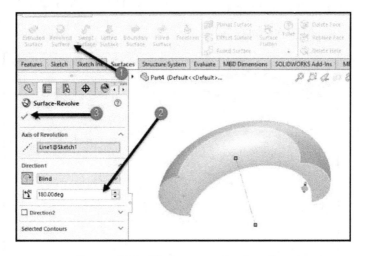

Figure 232 Click on revolved surface

Step 3: Click on ruled surface then select edges and specify distance.

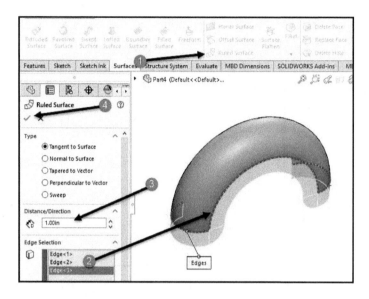

Figure 233 Specify distance

Note: Types of Ruled surface

1. **Tangent to surface**

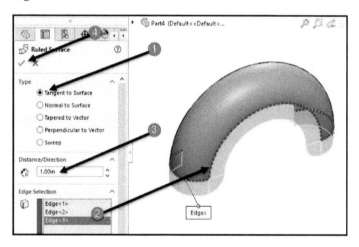

Figure 234   Tangent to surface

2. **Normal to surface**

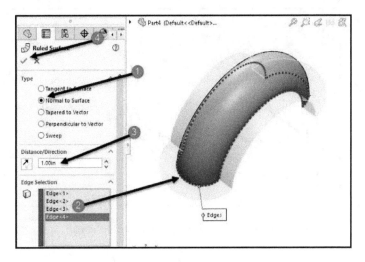

Figure 235 Normal to surface

3. **Tapered to vector**

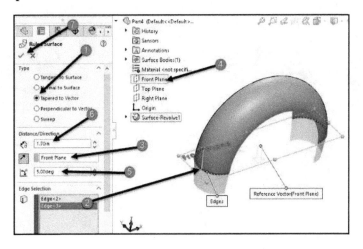

Figure 236 Tapered to vector

4. **Perpendicular to vector**

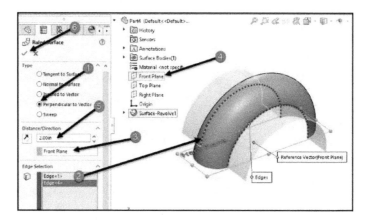

Figure 237 Perpendicular to vector

5. **Sweep**

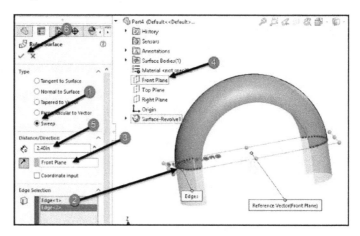

Figure 238 Sweep

Surface Flatten

Use Surface flatten tool to convert any made Surface model to a plane design. SolidWorks can any face, surface, or set of faces to create templates for manufacturing. This is useful when working with developable surfaces such as sheet metal parts with non-standard bends.

Step 1: Select surface then click on **Surface Flatten**.

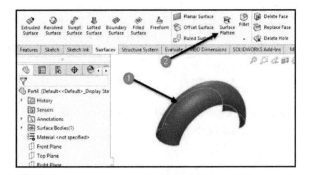

Figure 239 Surface flatten

Step 2: Pick on point.

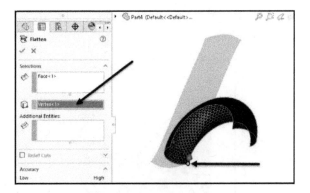

Figure 240 Pick on point

Step 3: Click on finish mode.

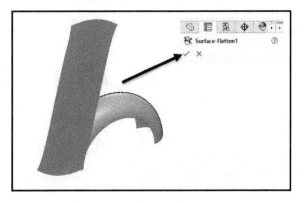

Figure 241 Finish mode

Delete Face

The main target of Delete Face is to delete faces, as you probably already could tell, based on the name of the feature. The command itself has three options to choose from:

Delete

Deletes a face from a surface body or deletes one or more faces from a solid body to create surfaces.

Delete and Patch

Deletes a face from a surface body or solid body and automatically patches and trims the body.

Delete and Fill

Deletes faces and generates a single face to close any gap.

Step 1: Create a solid box.

Figure 242 Solid box

Step 2: Click on **Delete Face** tool.

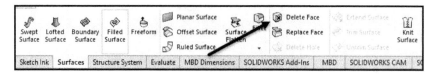

Figure 243 "delete face" tool

Step 3: Select face and **Delete** option.

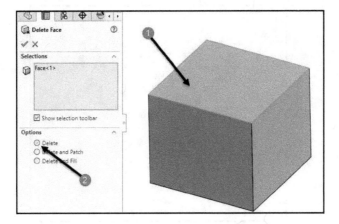

Figure 244 Select face and delete option

Step 4: Click on finish mode.

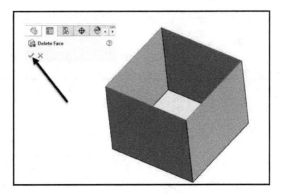

Figure 245 Click on finish mode

Replace Face

Use the replace surface tool to replace the solid body's face in another surface. The replacement surface body does not need to have the same boundaries as the old faces. When you replace a face, adjacent faces in the original body automatically extend and trim to the replacement surface body, and the new face trims.

Step 1: First, create a solid slot and a surface as given below.

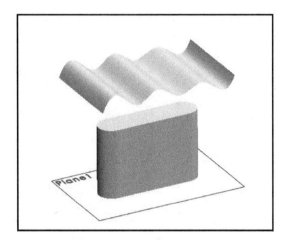

Figure 246 Create a solid slot and a surface

Step 2: Click on **Replace Face** tool.

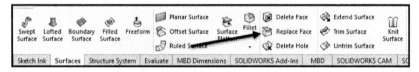

Figure 247 Click on "Replace face" tool

Step 3: Select target face and replacement surface.

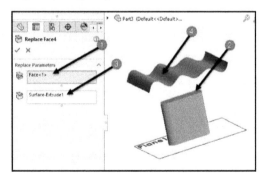

Figure 248 Select target face

Step 4: Click on finish mode.

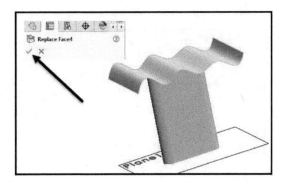

Figure 249 Click on finish mode

Extend Surface

Edge is the use of Surface Extend Tool to extend like Surface. The Surface Extend feature allows you. To take an existing surface and add material. In one or multiple directions. To get started we ought to make sure first. That we have a surface.

Step 1- First, Create a Surface.

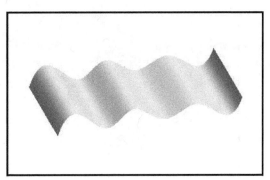

Figure 250 Create a Surface

Step 2- Click on **Extend Surface** tool.

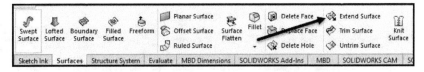

Figure 251 Click on "Extend surface" tool

Step 3: Select edge and specify distance.

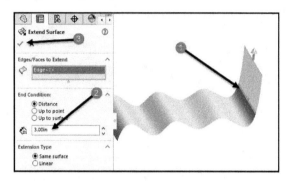

Figure 252 Select edge and specify distance

Trim Surface

Use trim surface to remove an extra part of the surface. To trim, there must be surface only.

Step 1: Create two different surfaces.

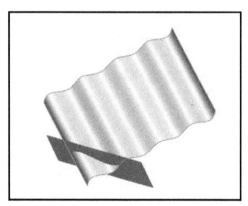

Figure 253 Create two different surfaces

Step 2: Click on **Trim surface** tool.

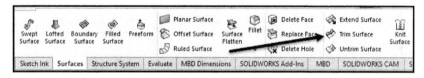

Figure 254 Trim surface

Step 3: Select trim tool and remove surface.

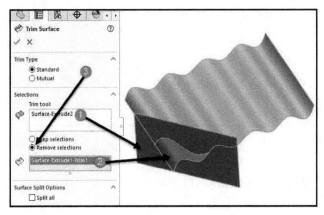

Figure 255 Select trim tool and remove surface

Step 4: Click on finish mode.

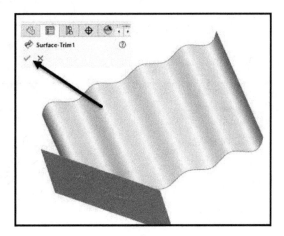

Figure 256 Click on finish mode

Untrim Surface

Use Untrim tool to bring back any trim part. This surface increases. With Untrim Surface, you can patch surface holes and external edges by extending an existing surface along its natural boundaries.

Step 1: A surface that is already made up.

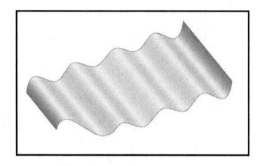

Figure 257 A surface

Step 2: Click on **Untrim surface** tool.

Figure 258 Untrim Surface

Step 3: Select face and click on finish.

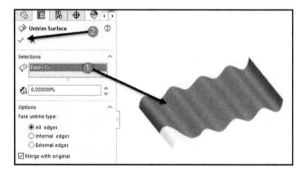

Figure 259 Click on finish

Knit Surface

Use knit surface tools to join two or more surface and fill the gap between them.

Step 1: First, make two surfaces. Both of which are different, as given below.

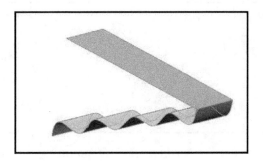

Figure 260 First make two surfaces

Step 2: Click on knit tool.

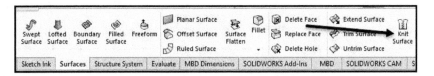

Figure 261 Click on knit tool

Step 3: Select both surface and click on finish mode.

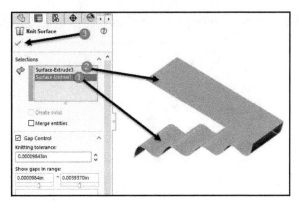

Figure 262 Select both surface

Note: Use Knit Tool to combine Surface. So that the surface thickness is equal to one.

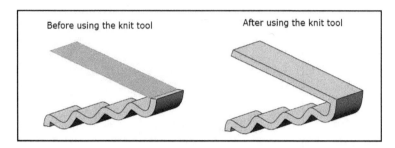

Figure 263 Different

Thicken

To convert Surface to body and to thicken surface, use surface thicken tool.

Step 1: Click on thicken tool.

Figure 264 Click on thicken tool

Step 2: Select surface and specify thickness.

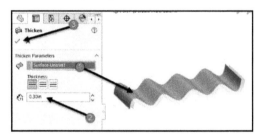

Figure 265 Specify thickness

CHAPTER 5

Sheet Metal

Base Flange/Tab

Use Base Flange Tool to create base flange of sheet metal. When you add a base flange feature to a SolidWorks part, the part is marked as a sheet metal part. Bends are added wherever appropriate, and sheet metal specific features are added to the Feature Manager design tree.

Step 1: Create a rectangle.

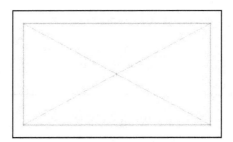

Figure 266 Create a rectangle

Step 2: Select sketch profile and click on **Base Flange** tool.

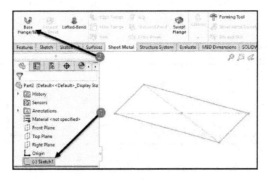

Figure 267 Base flange

Step 3: Specify sheet metal parameters, bend allowance and auto relief.

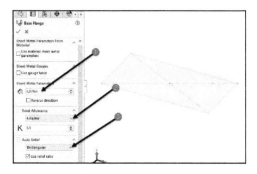

Figure 268 Bend allowance

Step 4: Click on finish mode.

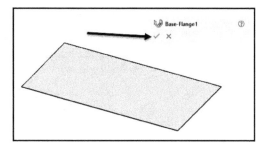

Figure 269 Finish mode

Edge Flange

When you add a base flange feature to a SolidWorks part, the part is marked as a sheet metal part. Bends are added wherever appropriate, and sheet metal specific features are added to the Feature Manager design tree.

Step 1: Click on **Edge Flange** tool.

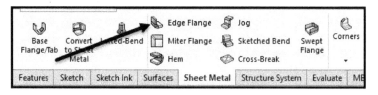

Figure 270 "edge flange" tool

Step 2: Select edge and specify all parameters. Such as flange radius, angle and length, and so on.

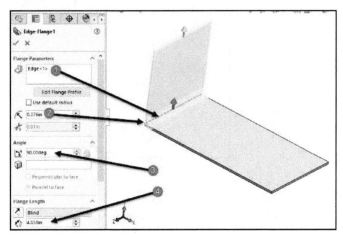

Figure 271 Specify all parameters

Step 3: Click on finish mode.

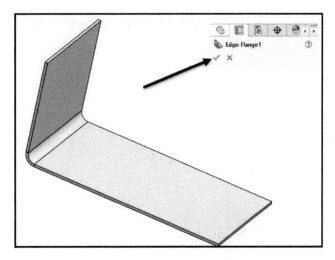

Figure 272 Finish mode

Note: If you want to change the flange width. So, click on the **Edit Flange Profile** button.

Step 1: Click on the edit flange profile button.

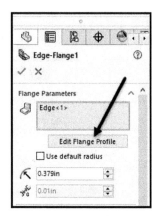

Figure 273 Edit Flange Profile button

Step 2: Change the profile from the help of dimension.

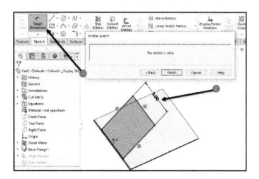

Figure 274 Change the profile

Step 3: After that, click on finish button.

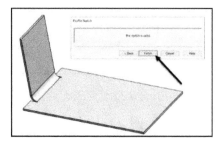

Figure 275 Finish button

Miter Flange

Miter flange is the same as edge flange. Just create flange in its own way. To create a miter flange, make a sketch inside the miter flange tool.

Step 1: Click on miter flange tool and pick on face.

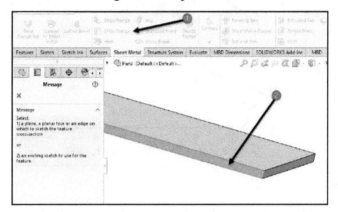

Figure 276 Click on miter flange tool

Step 2: Click on the line tool and create a sketch as given below. After that click on **Exit Sketch**.

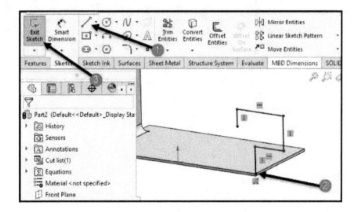

Figure 277 Click on line tool and create a sketch

Step 3: Specify all parameters then finish tool.

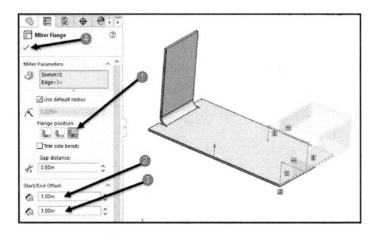

Figure 278 Specify all parameters

Hem

Use the hem tool to curve the edge of the flange. The hem tool adds a hem to your sheet metal part at a selected edge.

Step 1: Click on **Hem** tool and pick on face.

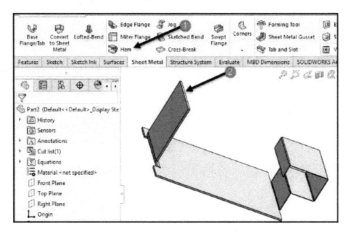

Figure 279 Click on hem tool

Step 2: Specify hem parameters.

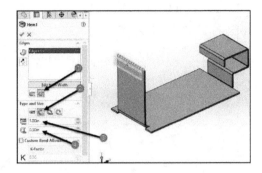

Figure 280 Specify hem parameters

Jog

To create a jog feature on a sheet metal part: Sketch a line on the face of a sheet metal part where you want to create the jog. Click Jog on the Sheet Metal toolbar or click **Insert | Sheet Metal | Jog**. In the graphics area, select a face for Fixed Face.

Step 1: Click on the jog tool and pick on face.

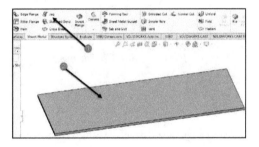

Figure 281 Click on jog tool

Step 2: Make a line and close the sketch profile.

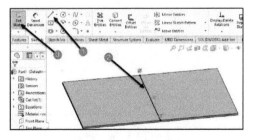

Figure 282 Sketch profile

Step 3: Click on jog tool and take offset distance.

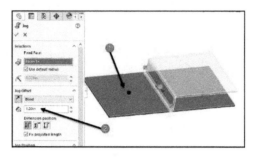

Figure 283 Take offset distance

Step 4: Click on finish mode.

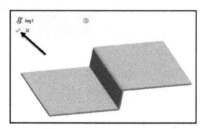

Figure 284 Finish mode

Sketched Bend

Use the sketched band tool to turn the flange on any angle.

Step 1: Click on **Sketched Bend** tool and pick on face.

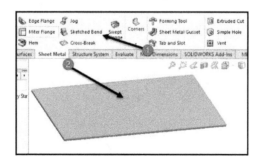

Figure 285 Sketched bend

Step 2: Make a line and close the sketch profile.

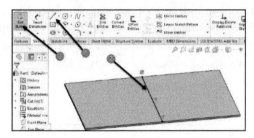

Figure 286 Sketch profile.

Step 3: Select base face and finish mode.

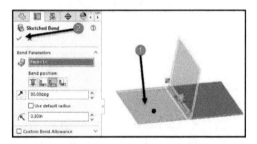

Figure 287 Finish mode

Cross-Break

The Cross-Break command lets you insert a graphical representation of a cross break in a sheet metal part.

Step 1: Click on **Cross-Break** tool and pick on face.

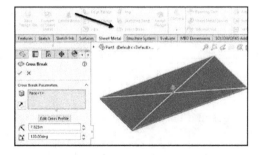

Figure 288 Cross-Break

Swept-flange

Swept Flange tool is like the Sweep tool. You need a profile and path to create the flange. To create a swept flange, you need an open profile sketch as the profile, and a sketch or a series of existing sheet metal edges as the path. These tools are like some miter flange tools.

Step 1: Create a base sheet and a profile sketch. As shown in the following screenshot:.

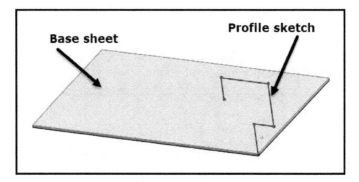

Figure 289 Create a base sheet and a profile sketch

Step 2: Click on swept flange tool and select profile sketch.

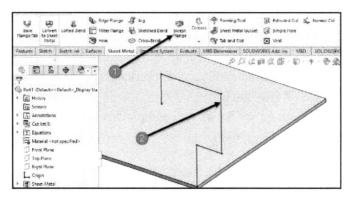

Figure 290 Swept flange tool

Step 3: Select edges and take radius.

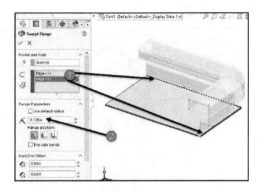

Figure 291 Select edges and take radius

Step 4: Click on finish mode.

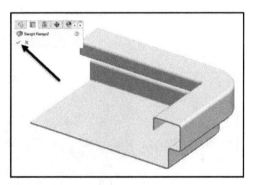

Figure 292 Finish mode

Closed Corner

Use the closed corner tool to fill the gap between two flanges. In the extend flange one side.

Step 1: Click on **Closed Corner** tool.

Figure 293 "Closed corner" tool

Step 2: Select face for extend.

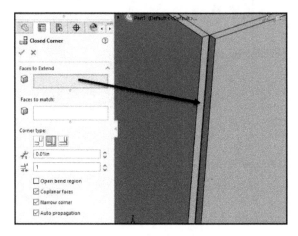

Figure 294 Select face

Step 3: Click on finish mode.

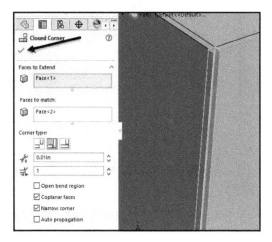

Figure 295 Finish mode

Welded Corner

Use the welded corner tool to fill the gap between two flanges. In this, the corner is welded.

Step 1: Click on **Welded Corner** tool.

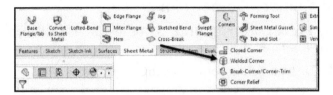

Figure 296 "welded corner" tool

Step 2: Select face for weld.

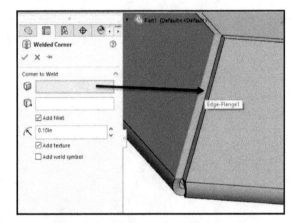

Figure 297 Select face for weld

Step 3: Click on finish mode.

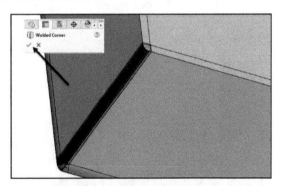

Figure 298 Click on finish mode

Break-Corner / Corner-Trim

Use the **Break-Corner / Corner-Trim** tool to make the corner of the flange a chamfer or fillet.

Step 1: Click on Break-Corner / Corner-Trim tool.

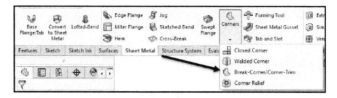

Figure 299 "Break corner/ Trim corner" tool

Step 2: Pick on edge of flange for corner trim.

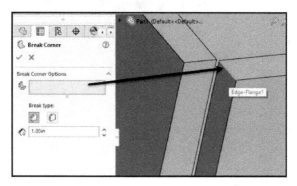

Figure 300 Pick on edge of flange

Step 3: Click on finish mode.

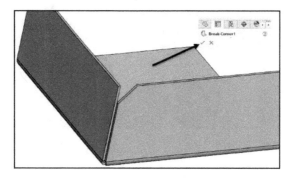

Figure 301 Click on finish mode

Corner Relief

You use the corner relief tool to change Corner's shape. You can apply corner treatments to a folded sheet metal body that will persist in the flattened state.

Step 1: Click on **Corner Relief** tool.

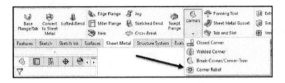

Figure 302 "Corner relief" tool

Step 2: Click on **Collect all corners** button.

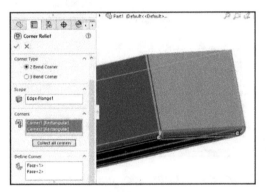

Figure 303 "Collect all corners" button.

Step 3: Click on finish mode.

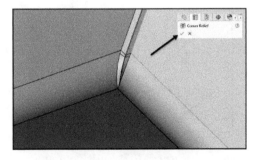

Figure 304 Click on finish mode

Sheet Metal Gusset

Use the Sheet metal gusset tool to support the sheet's flange. This is like a rib tool.

Step 1: Click on **Sheet Metal Gusset** tool.

Figure 305 "Sheet metal gusset" tool

Step 2: Select base face and vertical face for gusset. Then specify distance.

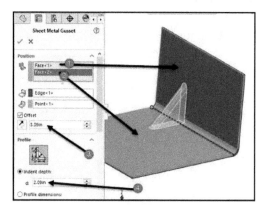

Figure 306 Select base face and vertical face for gusset

Step 3: Click on finish mode.

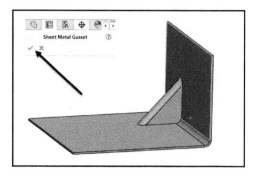

Figure 307 Finish mode

Vent

The Vent feature in SolidWorks is a great way to add any sort of vents for airflow through sheet metal and plastic parts. In this, any shape can be cut by sketch.

Step 1: Create a rectangle on base flange.

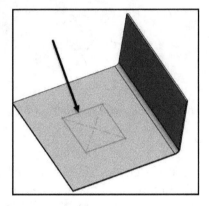

Figure 308 Create a rectangle

Step 2: Click on **Vent** tool.

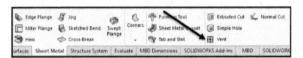

Figure 309 "Vent" tool

Step 3: Select all line of the rectangle.

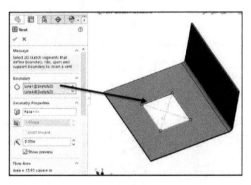

Figure 310 Select all line

Step 4: Select construction line for ribs.

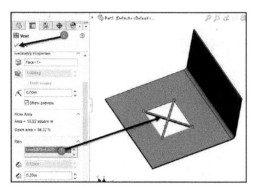

Figure 311 Select construction line

Tab and Slot

Tabs and slots make it easier to weld parts together and minimize the requirement to build complicated fixtures because you can interlock several sheet metal parts. This feature is available in all parts, not just sheet metal parts. You can use it in single body, multibody, and parts in the context of an assembly.

Step 1: Create a sheet metal design. As given in the following screenshot:

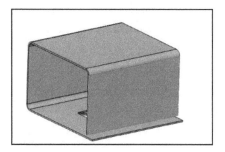

Figure 312 Create a sheet metal design

Step 2: Click on **Tab and Slot** tool.

Figure 313 "tab and slot" tool

Step 3: Select the **Blind** option, which is the height of the tabs.

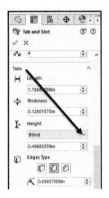

Figure 314 Select the blind option

Step 4: Select edge and face.

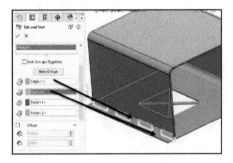

Figure 315 Select edge and face

Step 5: Specify height, length, radius and tab numbers.

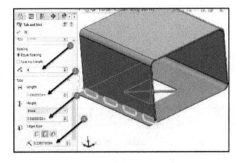

Figure 316 Specify height

Unfold

The sheet which is already bend. Use the unfold tool to remove its band.

Step 1: Click on **Unfold"** tool.

Figure 317 "unfold" tool

Step 2: Select base flange and click on **Collect All Bends** button.

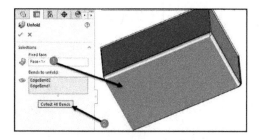

Figure 318 "collect all bends" button

Step 3: Click on finish mode.

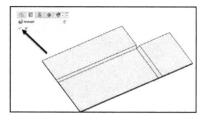

Figure 319 Finish mode

Fold

Use the fold tool to fold the unfold sheet.

Step 1: Click on **Fold** tool.

Figure 320 "Fold" tool

Step 2: Select the base face and click on **Collect All Bends** button.

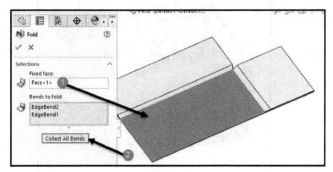

Figure 321 "Collect all bends" button

Step 3: Click on finish mode.

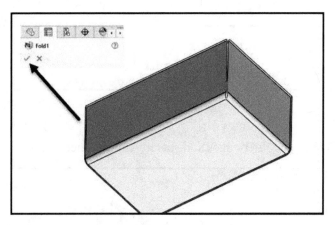

Figure 322 Finish mode

Rip

When a body has to convert it to sheet meteal. Then use the rip tool to give it a gap in the bend.

Step 1: First, make a box with the use of the extrude and shell tool.

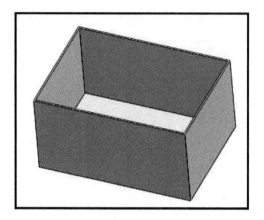

Figure 323 Use of the extrude and shell tool

Step 2: Click on **Rip** tool.

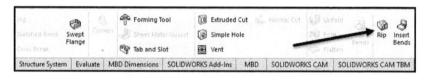

Figure 324 "Rip" tool

Step 3: Select corner edges and specify gap distance.

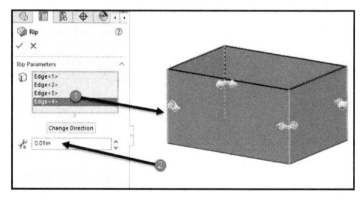

Figure 325 Specify gap distance

Step 4: Click on finish mode.

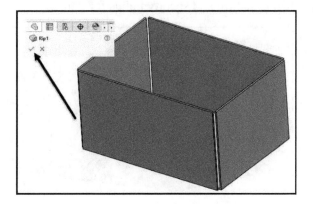

Figure 326 Finish mode

Insert Bends

The insert bend is used to insert bands on the sheet.

Step 1: First, click on **Insert Bends** tool.

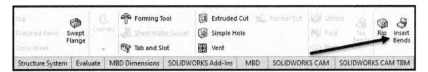

Figure 327 "Insert bends" tool

Step 2: Select base face and specify radius for flange.

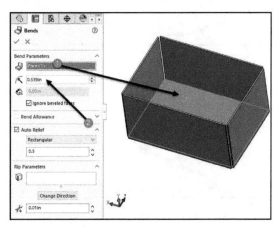

Figure 328 Specify radius for flange

Step 3: Select base face and specify radius for flange.

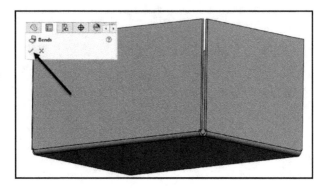

Figure 329 Specify radius for flange

Forming Tool

To insert punch design in sheet, the punch design that is made. For him, use the forming tool.

Step 1: First, create a solid body.

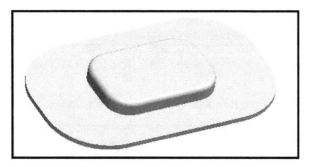

Figure 330 Create a solid body

Step 2: Click on **Forming** tool.

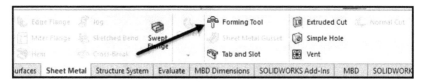

Figure 331 Forming Tool

Step 3: Select face for stopping face.

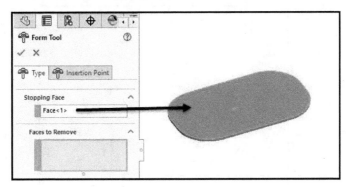

Figure 332 Stopping Face

Lofted-bend

Use the lofted bend tool to create a sheet of different sketches on different planes.

Step 1: Make a sketch on Rectangle and Circle on one.

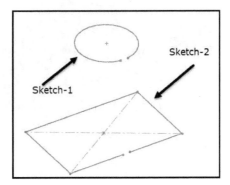

Figure 333 Rectangle and Circle

Step 2: Click on **Lofted-Bend** tool.

Figure 334 "Lofted-bend" tool

Step 3: Select sketch 1 and 2.

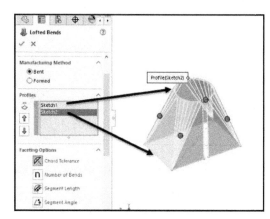

Figure 335 Sketch 1 and 2

Step 4: Click on finish tool.

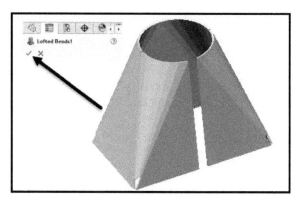

Figure 336 Finish mode

CHAPTER 6
Weldments

Weldments

The weldments tool is used to convert structural section into weldment.

Step 1: Click on **Weldments** tool.

Figure 337 "Weldments" tool

Structural Member

Use the structural frame tool to make steel frames.

Step 1: Create a 3D sketch.

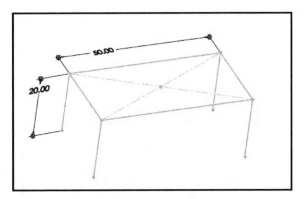

Figure 338 Create a 3D sketch.

Step 2: Click on **Structural Member** tool.

Figure 339 "Structural Member" tool

Step 3: Select steel standard, type, and size.

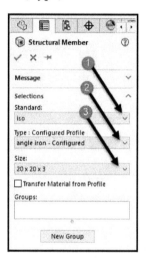

Figure 340 Select steel standard

Step 3: Select lines.

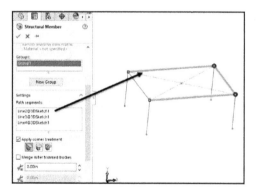

Figure 341 Select lines

Step 4: Click on finish mode.

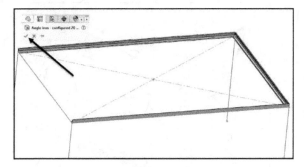

Figure 342 Finish mode

Trim/Extend

The gap between steel in the structural frame is that gap. Two segments at a corner where they meet. Use the Trim/Extend tool to add them.

Step 1: Click on **Trim/Extend** tool.

Figure 343 "Trim/Extend" tool

Step 2: Select corner type. Then select iron angle.

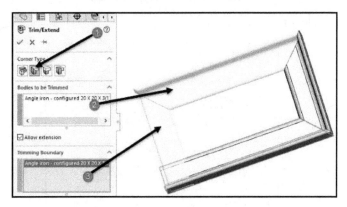

Figure 344 Select iron angle

Step 3: Click on finish mode.

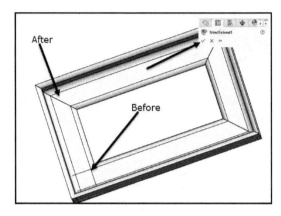

Figure 345 Finish mode

End Cap

It is use. Capping an outer surface at one end. You can cap an outer surface at one end or at both ends.

Step 1: Click on **End Cap** tool.

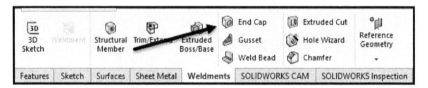

Figure 346 "End cap" tool

Step 2: Select face for cap end.

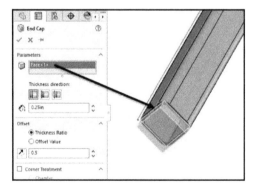

Figure 347 Select face for cap end

Gusset

This is similar to the Rib Tool. These frames are used in between two steel so that both of them could be supported.

Step 1: Click on **Gusset** tool.

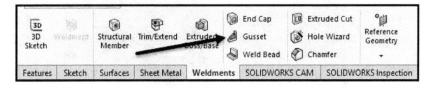

Figure 348 "Gusset" tool

Step 2: Select supporting faces.

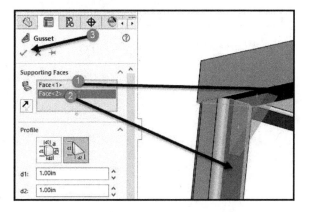

Figure 349 Select supporting faces

Weld Bead

Use the weld bald tool to weld the frame.

Step 1: Click on **Weld bead** tool.

Figure 350 "Weld bead" tool

Step 2: Click on **Smart weld selection** tool. Then select the faces through the drag.

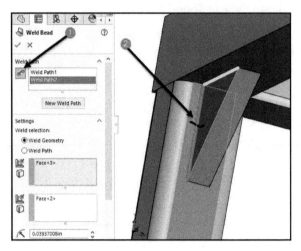

Figure 351 "Smart weld selection" tool

CHAPTER 7
Curves

Split Line

Using the split line tool to cut the solid body through the line sketch.

Step 1: First, create a cylinder profile.

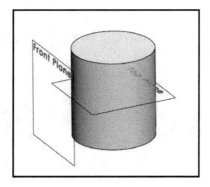

Figure 352 Create a cylinder profile.

Step 2: Create a spline.

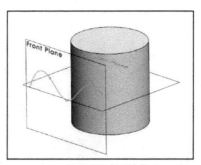

Figure 353 Create a spline.

Step 3: Click on **Split Line** tool.

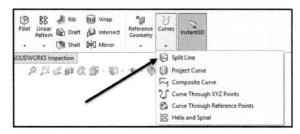

Figure 354 "Split Line" tool

Step 4: Select spline for projected and face for split.

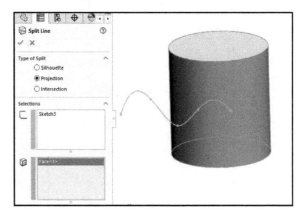

Figure 355 Select spline for projected and face for split

Step 5: Click on finish mode.

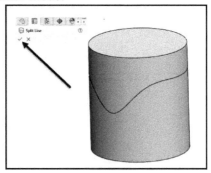

Figure 356 Finish mode

Project Curves

If two different sketches have to be got a new sketch. Or a sketch should be printed on a body. So, use the projected curves tool.

Step 1: First, create two sketches where first is circle and second is arc.

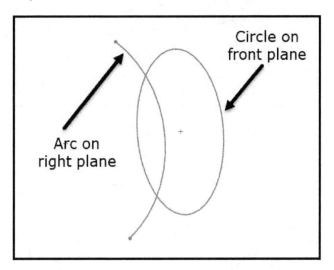

Figure 357 Create two sketches

Step 2: Click on **Project Curve** tool.

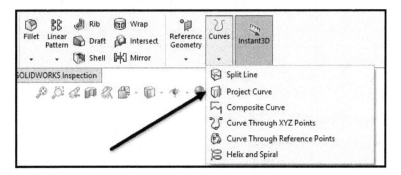

Figure 358 "Project Curve" tool

Step 3: Select arc and circle.

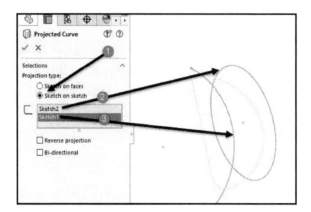

Figure 359 Select arc and circle

Step 4: Click on finish mode.

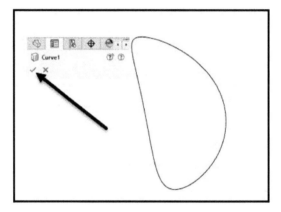

Figure 360 Finish mode

Curve through XYZ Points

When it involves complex entities in SolidWorks 2019, we usually use the spline tool. However, in the case of parabolic curves or involute the spline tool may not give us the accuracy and flexibility we need for a particular geometry.

Step 1: Click on **Curve Through XYZ Points** tool.

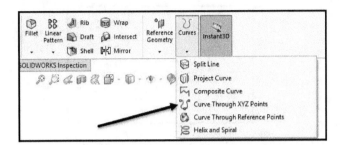

Figure 361 "Curve Through XYZ Points" tool

Step 2: Specify XYZ value.

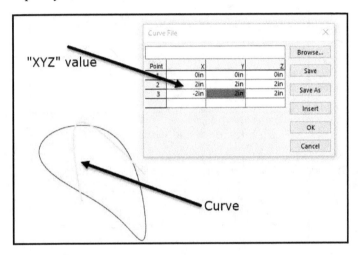

Figure 362 Specify xyz value

Helix and Spiral

Use the helix spiral tool to create a spring or ring shape. You can create a helix or spiral curve in a part. In a part, do one of the following: Open a sketch and sketch a circle. Select a sketch that contains a circle.

Step 1: First, create a circle for helix base.

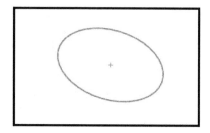

Figure 363 Create a circle

Step 2: Select circle then click on **Helix and Spiral** tool.

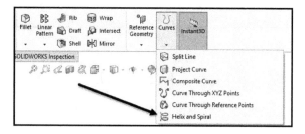

Figure 364 "Helix and Spiral" tool

Step 3: Specify parameters such as pitch and revolutions.

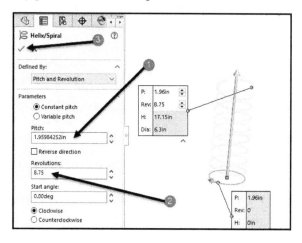

Figure 365 Specify parameters

Composite Curve

Use the composite curve tool to make the normal sketch and helix one segment.

Step 1: Make a helix, after that, make a sketch of the hook type.

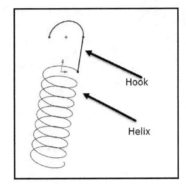

Figure 366 Make a helix and a hook

Step 2: Finish sketch then click on **Composite Curve** tool.

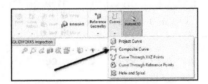

Figure 367 "Composite Curve" tool

Step 3: Select hook sketch and helix.

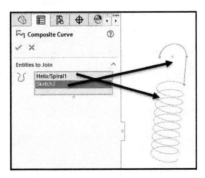

Figure 368 Hook sketch and helix

Step 4: Click on finish mode.

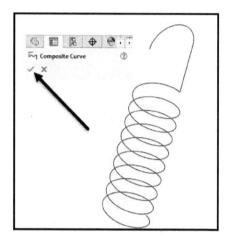

Figure 369 Finish mode

Curve through Reference Point

Curve Through Reference Points creates a curve through points located on one or more planes. Click on **Curve Through Reference Points** on the **Curves** toolbar, or click on **Insert**, **Curve**, **Curve Through Reference Points**.

Step 1: Click on **Curve Through Reference Point** tool.

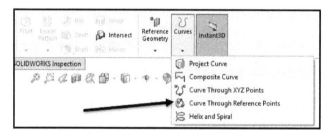

Figure 370 "Curve Through Reference Point" tool

Step 2: Pick on vertex.

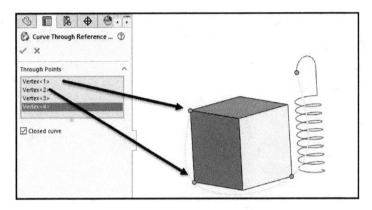

Figure 371 Pick on vertex

Step 3: Click on finish mode.

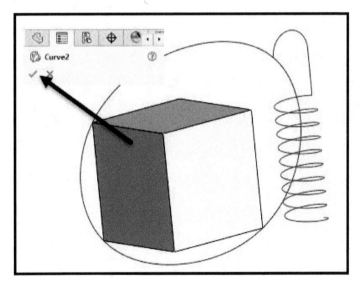

Figure 372 Finish mode

CHAPTER 8
Mold Design

Parting Lines

Parting lines lie along the edge of the moulded part, between the core and the cavity surfaces. They are used to create the parting surfaces and to separate the surfaces. You create the parting lines after the model is scaled and a proper draft is applied.

Step 1: First, create one side open cylinder.

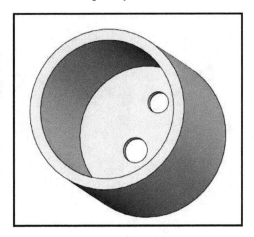

Figure 373 Create one side open cylinder

Step 2: Click on **Parting Lines** tool.

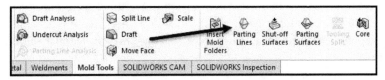

Figure 374 "Parting Lines" tool

Step 3: Select the face of the pull direction. Then click on **Draft Analysis** button and select parting line.

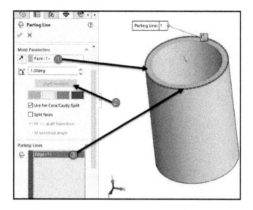

Figure 375 "Draft Analysis" button

Step 4: Click on finish mode.

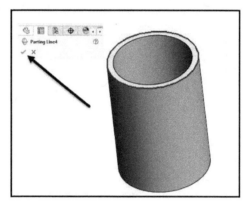

Figure 376 finish mode

Parting Surface

You can create a parting surface, which is extruded from parting lines, to separate the mold cavity from the core. You must create a parting surface to create a tooling split. To make a parting surface, it must be a parting line.

Step 1: To make a parting surface, it is important to have a parting line. Which is made from the parting line tool.

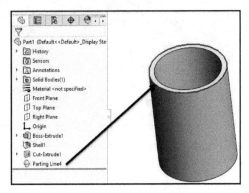

Figure 377 Parting Line

Step 2 Click on **Parting surface** tool.

Figure 378 "Parting Surface" tool

Step 3: Select parting line and specify surface distance.

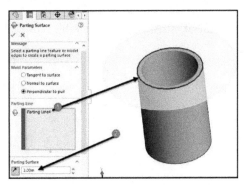

Figure 379 Specify surface distance

Step 4: Click on finish mode.

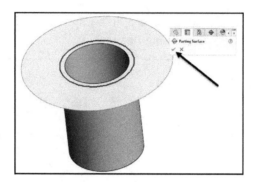

Figure 380 Finish mode

Shut Off Surface

To cut a tooling block into pieces, you need two complete surfaces without any through holes. Shut-off surfaces close the through holes. You create shut-off surfaces after creating the parting lines.

Step 1: Shut off surface.

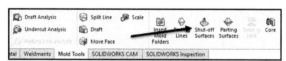

Figure 381 Shut off

Step 2: To use a shut off surface, make a solid part. Which should have a hole.

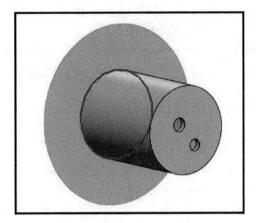

Figure 382 Make a solid part

Step 3: Click on **Shut-off Surface** tool.

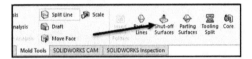

Figure 383 "Shut-off Surface" tool

Step 4: When you click on the tool, it automatically selects the open edges.

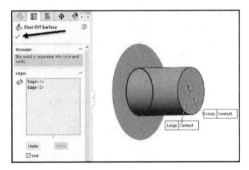

Figure 384 Selects the open edges

Tooling Split

Core and cavity require tooling split tools. To create a tooling split, the part must have at least three surface bodies in the Surface Bodies.

Step 1: Click on **Tooling Split** tool.

Figure 385 "Tooling Split" tool

Step 2: Pick on surface and click on rectangle tool.

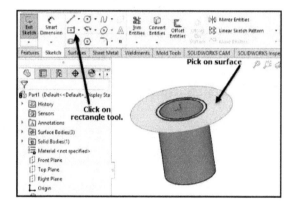

Figure 386 Click on rectangle tool

Step 3: Create rectangle then click on finish sketch.

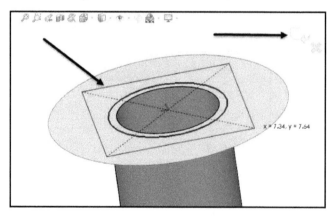

Figure 387 Finish sketch.

Step 4: Specify block size and click on finish mode.

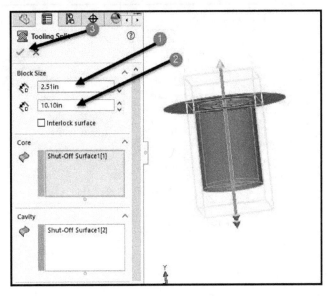

Figure 388 Specify block size

Step 4: Right click on part configuration and click on new exploded view.

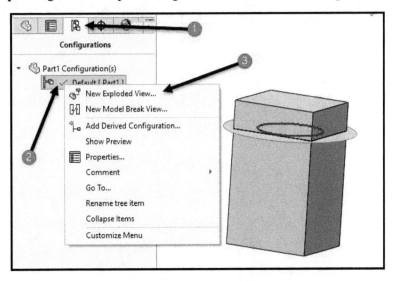

Figure 389 New exploded view

Step 5: Select core and cavity one by one. Then drag by y axis.

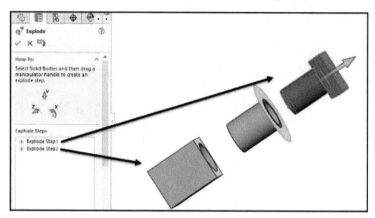

Figure 390 Drag by y axis

CHAPTER 9

Assembly

Insert Components

Use the insert component tool to bring the part to the assembly.

Step 1: Open assembly page.

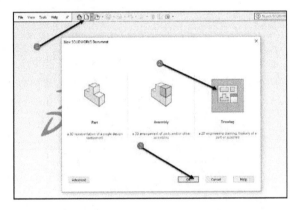

Figure 391 Open page

Step 2: Click on **Insert Components** tool.

Figure 392 "Insert Components" tool

Step 3: Click on **Browser** button. Then select file and click on **Open** button.

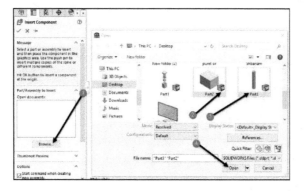

Figure 393 Click on Browser button

Step 4: Click on screen for insert component.

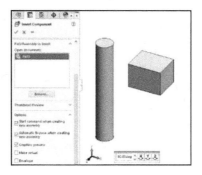

Figure 394 Insert

Mate

Use the mate tool to combine the part in the assembly. There are many types of mate.

Step 1: Click on **Mate** tool.

Figure 395 Click on mate

Step 2: Pick face of box and again pick face of cylinder.

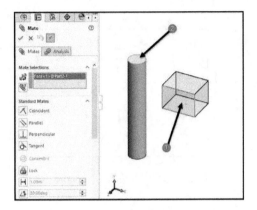

Figure 396 Select face

Step 3: The Mate tools will automatically add both faces.

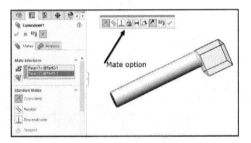

Figure 397 Set mate

Step 4: Click on **View temporary axis**.

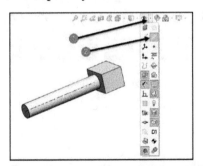

Figure 398 View temporary axis

Step 4: Again click on mate tool. Then select temporary axis and face of box.

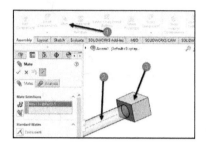

Figure 399 Select axis and face

Step 5: Click on **Distance mate**. Then specify distance and finish.

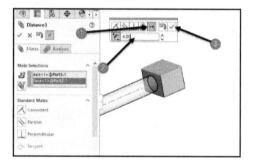

Figure 400 Distance mate

Step 6: Following are some mate tool options.

Figure 401 Mate option

1. Coincident
2. Parallel
3. Perpendicular
4. Fix

5. Dimension

6. Angel

7. Reverse direction

8. Undo

9. Finish

Edit Components

If there is modification in assembly doing time part. So, use the edit component tool.

Step 1: Select the part which you want to edit. Then click on **Edit Components** button.

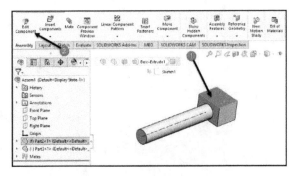

Figure 402 Edit component

Step 2: Click on **Fillet** tool.

Figure 403 Click on fillet

Step 3: Select edges and then specify fillet radius.

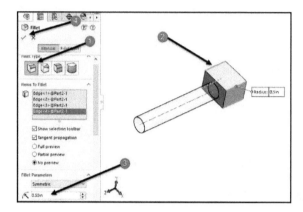

Figure 404 Specify fillet

Step 4: Click on exit component.

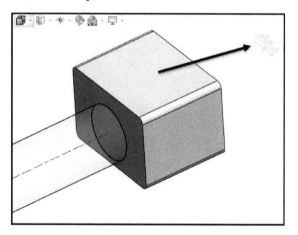

Figure 405 Exit

Smart Fasteners

If the Hole Wizard has already been used in the body. So, use Smart fasteners tools to create screws apply in it.

Step 1: First make a plate, use the Hole Wizard then open this plate in the assembly.

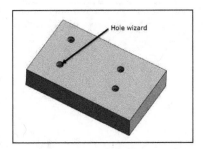

Figure 406 Hole wizard

Step 2: Click on **Toolbox** button then click on **Add in now** button.

Figure 407 Toolbox

Step 3: Click on smart fasteners tool.

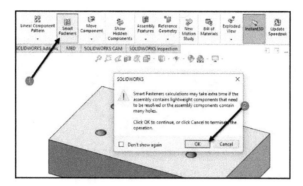

Figure 408 Smart fasteners

Step 4: Select the face of hole wizard then click add button.

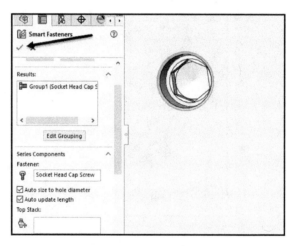

Figure 409 Use smart fasteners

Move Component

Use the move component tool for the displacement of the part.

Step 1: By selecting the part. By right-clicking on it Then click on the Fix button. If there is no fix button, then the part is already float.

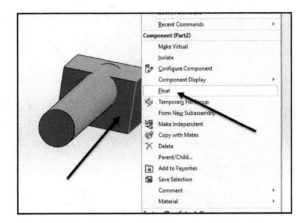

Figure 410 Change fix to float

Step 2: Click on move component.

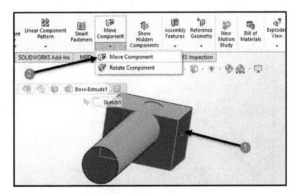

Figure 411 Move component

Step 3: Select move type.

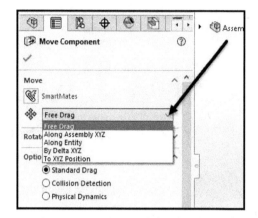

Figure 412 Move type

Rotate Component

To rotate the part, use the rotate component tool.

Step 1: Select part then click on **Rotate Component** tool.

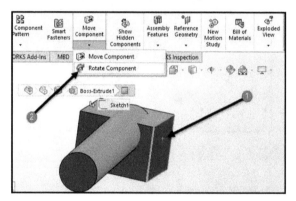

Figure 413 Rotate component

Step 2: Select rotate type.

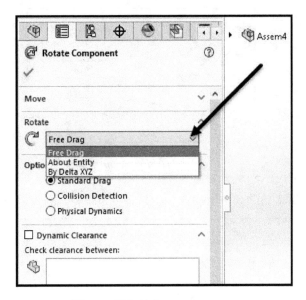

Figure 414 Select rotate type

Cavity

Use the cavity tool to cut the other part through one part.

Step 1: Create a box and cylinder.

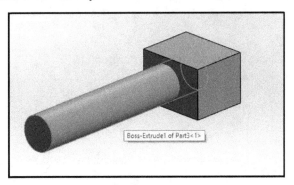

Figure 415 Box and cylinder for cavity

Step 2: Select box and click on edit component.

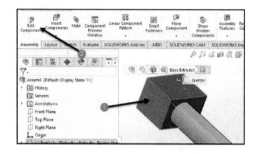

Figure 416 Edit component

Step 3: Click on cavity tool.

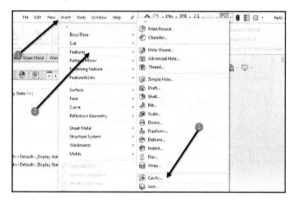

Figure 417 Cavity

Step 4: Select cylinder then specify parameters.

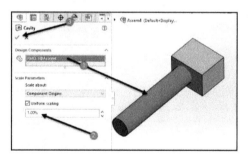

Figure 418 Specify scale

Step 5: Hide cylinder then click on exit.

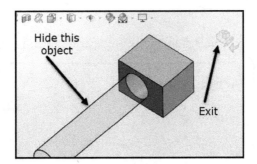

Figure 419 Exit

Step 6: Final cavity part.

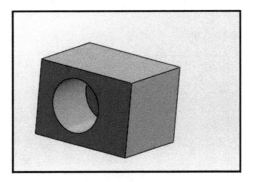

Figure 420 Cavity

Join

Use the join tool to combine the two parts.

Step 1: Open assembly then browse two part.

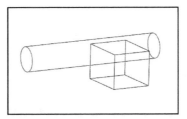

Figure 421 Open assembly

Step 2: Select cylinder then click on edit component.

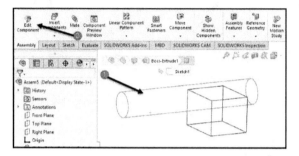

Figure 422 Edit component

Step 3: Click on join tool.

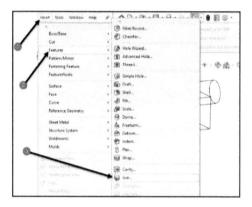

Figure 423 Join tool

Step 4: Select box.

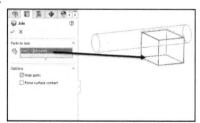

Figure 424 Select box

Step 5: Click on finish mode.

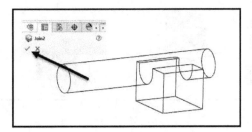

Figure 425 Finish mode.

Belt/Chain

Use the Belt/Chain assembly feature to model of belts and chains and sprockets. The Belt/Chain assembly feature creates Belt mates to constrain the relative rotation of the pulley components. A sketch containing a closed chain of arcs and lines describing the path of the belt.

Step 1: Open assembly page then browse two wheels.

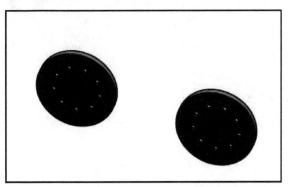

Figure 426 Two wheels

Step 2: Click on belt/chain tool.

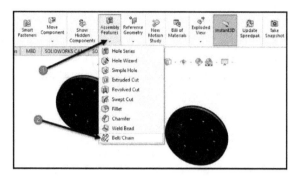

Figure 427 Belt chain

Step 3: Select circular faces then click on finish mode.

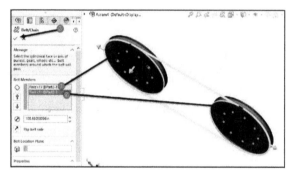

Figure 428 Select face

Exploded View

The separation of the assemble is to do it by Exploded view.

Step 1: Open assemble drawing.

Figure 429 Open assemble drawing

Step 2: Click on **Exploded View** tool.

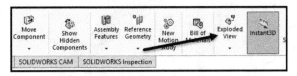

Figure 430 Exploded view

Step 3: Select part and drag. Then click on **Done** button.

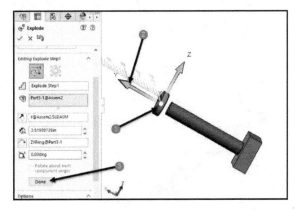

Figure 431 Drag part

Step 4: Again select second part and drag. Then click on **Done** button.

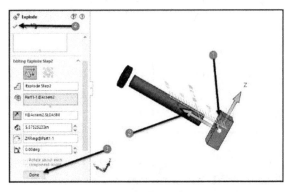

Figure 432 Second part drag

Step 5: Click on animate collapse in exploded view.

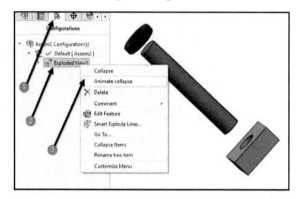

Figure 433 Animate collapse

Step 6: Set animation controller.

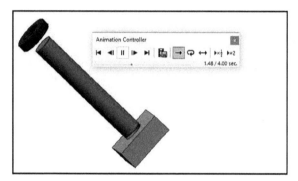

Figure 434 Animation controller

Bill of Materials

The use of bill of material to show the details of all the parts used in the assembly.

Step 1: Click on **Bill of Materials** tool.

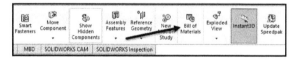

Figure 435 Bill of materials

Step 2: Select option then select **OK**.

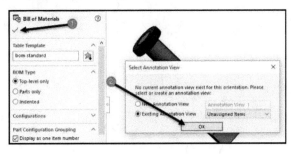

Figure 436 Annotation view

Step 3: Select table column then right click. And click insert then click column right.

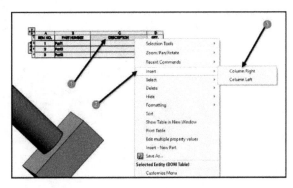

Figure 437 Insert column

Step 4: Select the column type.

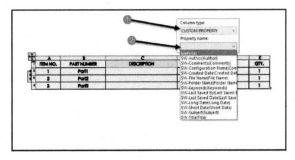

Figure 438 Column type

CHAPTER 10

Drafting

Select Sheet Format

Step 1: Open the drawing page.

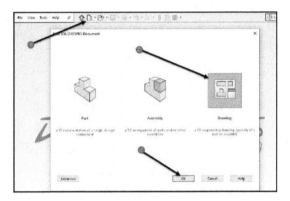

Figure 439 Open drawing page

Step 2: Select page then click **OK**.

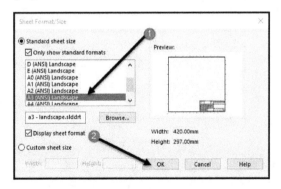

Figure 440 Select page

Step 3: Click browse button and select part. Then click open button.

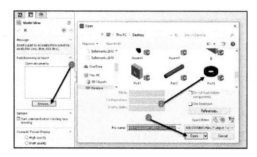

Figure 441 Open part

Step 4: Place part and select visual style.

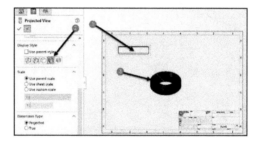

Figure 442 Place part

Standard 3 View

Step 1: Click on **Standard 3 View** button and click on browse button. Then select part and open.

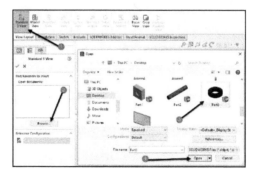

Figure 443 Standard view

Step 2: Click on page.

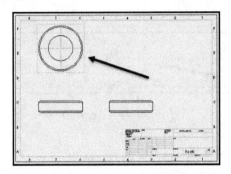

Figure 444 Click on page

Projected View

Step 1: Click on projected view.

Figure 445 Projected view

Step 2: Select part then drag.

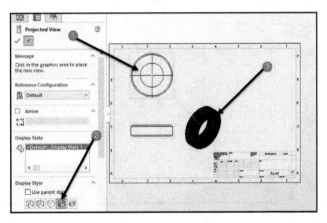

Figure 446 Drag part

Section View

Step 1: Click on section view tool.

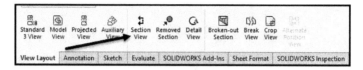

Figure 447 Section view

Step 2: Select section type then pick point.

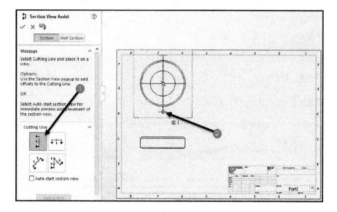

Figure 448 Section type

Step 3: Then click on finish.

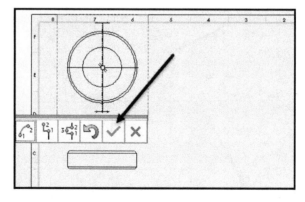

Figure 449 finish

Step 4: Specify position.

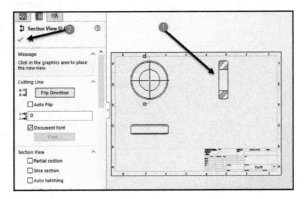

Figure 450 Specify position

Detail View

Step 1: Click on **Detail View** tool.

Figure 451 Detail view

Step 2: Create circle.

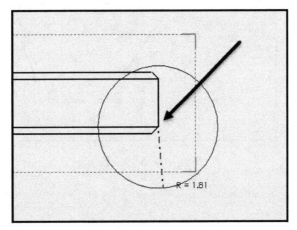

Figure 452 Mark area

Step 3: Then specify position.

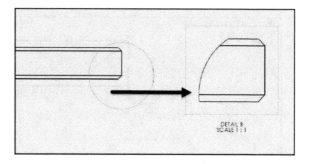

Figure 453 Specify position

Model Items

Step 1: Click on model items tool.

Figure 454 Click model items

Step 2: Select part.

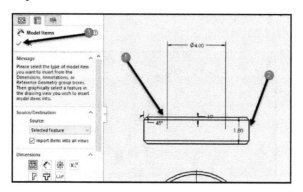

Figure 455 Select part

www.ingramcontent.com/pod-product-compliance
Lightning Source LLC
LaVergne TN
LVHW080116070326
832902LV00015B/2609